Rainer Werner
Fassbinder

Rainer Werner *Fassbinder*

Edited by Laurence Kardish, in collaboration with Juliane Lorenz

THE MUSEUM OF MODERN ART, NEW YORK

Distributed by Harry N. Abrams, Inc., New York

Published in conjunction with the exhibition *Rainer Werner Fassbinder,*
organized by Laurence Kardish, Curator and Coordinator of Film Exhibitions,
The Museum of Modern Art, New York, January 23–March 20, 1977.

This exhibition is supported in part by a grant from Christoph Henkel.

Transportation is provided by Lufthansa, Berlin.

Produced by the Department of Publications
The Museum of Modern Art, New York
Osa Brown, Director of Publications
Edited by Christopher Lyon and Barbara Ross
Designed by Jim Hinchee Design
Production by Cynthia Ehrhardt
Printed by Science Press, Ephrata, Pennsylvania
Bound by Mueller Trade Bindery, Middletown, Connecticut

"A Cinema of Vicious Circles" © 1997 by Thomas Elsaesser
"'A Very Sad Song Sung with Lots of Feeling'" © 1997 by Georgia Brown

Library of Congress Catalogue Card Number 96-79309
ISBN 0-87070-109-6 (MoMA, T&H)
ISBN 0-8109-6170-9 (Abrams)

Published by The Museum of Modern Art, 11 West 53 Street, New York, N.Y. 10019

Distributed in the United States and Canada by Harry N. Abrams, Inc., New York,
A Times Mirror Company

Distributed outside the United States and Canada by Thames and Hudson, Ltd.,
London

Printed in the United States of America

Cover and p.41: RWF, 1980
Frontispiece: *Fox and His Friends.* 1974. RWF

Contents

RWF on the set of
Lili Marleen, 1980

Foreword

Rainer Werner Fassbinder was born in Bad Wörishofen, Germany, on May 31, 1945, fifty years after motion pictures were first projected, and barely three weeks after the Third Reich surrendered to the Allied Forces. Cinema was well-established as a popular art, and Germany had yet to reinvent itself.

Twenty-one years later, Fassbinder made his first film (a short, now lost), and in the thirteen years following he completed forty-three more. These films reconfigured the grammar of cinema and charted, with a passionate ferocity, the nature of contemporary German society. Although his was a nation in which the cultural divide between generations was as wide as servility is from dissent, Fassbinder, with acute psychological insight, located the universal in the idiosyncratic behavior of his protagonists. Thus, as grounded as the filmmaker was in his native Germany, his works instantly illuminated the lives of audiences the world over. Prolific and ever able to astonish, Fassbinder emerged as one of the major artists of the late twentieth century.

The Museum of Modern Art is pleased and honored to have worked with the Rainer Werner Fassbinder Foundation in Berlin to present a complete retrospective of the director's films for the first time in the United States.

For this retrospective, the foundation, under the direction of Juliane Lorenz, has made over fifteen new, subtitled 35mm prints, and in many cases has restored the color faded from the original 16mm reversal prints. The foundation has also made possible as part of the retrospective the first showing, in any cinema, of Fassbinder's 1973 science-fiction drama *Welt am Draht (World on a Wire)*, originally adapted for television from the novel by Daniel F. Galouyé. Americans will also have a chance to see the "radical" or "German" ending to *Mutter Küsters' Fahrt zum Himmel (Mother Küsters Goes to Heaven)*, in addition to the "soft" or "American" ending that Fassbinder originally wrote for the film. We are grateful to Juliane Lorenz, who was Fassbinder's editor and companion, not only for making this extraordinary retrospective possible but also for her collaboration on this catalogue.

Lastly, I would like to extend my sincere thanks to Larry Kardish, Curator and Coordinator of Film Exhibitions, Department of Film and Video, for his tireless work on this important project. Without his dedication and effort, this retrospective and its accompanying publication would not have come to fruition.

Glenn D. Lowry
Director
The Museum of Modern Art

Preface

For the first time, The Museum of Modern Art in New York is making it possible to see the filmic work of Rainer Werner Fassbinder in its entirety: forty-one feature films and two shorts, among them multipart television films. If one could see this oeuvre in a single sitting, there would be 126 hours of film—nonstop movies for five days and six hours. In these films the audience will encounter a time period in Germany between 1966 and 1982. In spite of the fact that Fassbinder's creative life lasted only sixteen years, terminated by his early death at thirty-seven, the spirit of that work is not bound by any time.

Not only did Rainer Werner Fassbinder leave us a legacy of forty-three films, fourteen plays, four radio dramas, and a number of essays, he also left one of the most varied and most discussed bodies of artistic work in German postwar history. This work asks for responsible care. In 1986, Liselotte Eder, Fassbinder's mother, founded a private, not-for-profit foundation whose aim is the preservation and dissemination of the artistic work of Rainer Werner Fassbinder. From 1976 to 1982, I had the privilege of accompanying Rainer in his private and professional life, and I am fully aware of the responsibility toward an artist of such standing, and toward his work. In 1992, I assumed the directorship of the foundation.

Since then, the Rainer Werner Fassbinder Foundation has been active in the conservation and distribution of the films. Rights issues have been resolved, film negatives and copies secured, films reconstructed, and the groundwork laid to create an archive. The highlight of the foundation's work thus far is the event that this publication accompanies. The fact that the Department of Film and Video of The Museum of Modern Art has engaged in this first all-encompassing retrospective in the United States, and has put its trust in the Fassbinder Foundation, fills me with gratitude, pride, and a measure of self-confidence. We are certain that the work of Rainer Werner Fassbinder deserves this important showcase, and we wish our American audience stimulating hours of viewing, discovering or rediscovering his films.

My special thanks to Mary Lea Bandy, Laurence Kardish, and Ingrid Scheib-Rothbart.

Juliane Lorenz
Director
Rainer Werner Fassbinder Foundation, Berlin

Pioniere in Ingolstadt
(Recruits in Ingolstadt).
1971. Hanna Schygulla,
Günther Kaufmann

RWF, Karl Scheydt on the
set of *Warnung vor einer
heiligen Nutte (Beware of
a Holy Whore)*, 1970

Introduction

The first newspaper review of a Fassbinder film in New York, and perhaps the United States, was Vincent Canby's favorable notice of *Recruits in Ingolstadt*. It was the ninth feature-length film Rainer Werner Fassbinder had made in two years, and the earliest shown at the New York Film Festival. Fassbinder, who had trained as an actor, tried unsuccessfully in 1966 to enter the recently established German Film and Television Academy in Berlin. In 1967 he joined a Munich "basement theater" group, whose space was soon closed by the police; his colleagues and he immediately created another group, the antiteater, for which he wrote, directed, and acted. It was with antiteater members, including Irm Hermann, Kurt Raab, Peer Raben, and Hanna Schygulla, that Fassbinder began making feature films the following year. In *The New York Times* (October 11, 1971) Canby described with his customary perspicaciousness the mood of *Recruits in Ingolstadt* as "comic melancholia" inflected by Brechtian theatrical strategy. A curious and affecting tension between realism of location and costume, and artifice of performance and makeup, suggested the characters' interior drama while it intensified the surface one.

Over the next six years Fassbinder made fourteen films, and every autumn Richard Roud, of the New York Film Festival, would show one: in 1972, *The Merchant of Four Seasons*; in 1973, *The Bitter Tears of Petra Von Kant*; in 1974, *Ali: Fear Eats the Soul*; in 1975, *Fox and His Friends*; and in 1976, *Fear of Fear*. Meanwhile, museum film programs, like those at The Museum of Modern Art, New York, or the Pacific Film Archive, University Art Museum, Berkeley, would include the occasional Fassbinder film in various German series, and the pioneering distributor-exhibitor Daniel Talbot, under his New Yorker Films banner, would provide theatrical engagements for Fassbinder films that had premiered at the New York Film Festival.

Even though Fassbinder's reputation as a major contemporary filmmaker was growing, accessibility to his works was limited.

In 1977, after Fassbinder had completed twenty-two theatrical films, Americans could see twelve of these thanks to New Yorker Films' traveling exhibition *Fassbinder—The First Major Festival*. Even for those of us already impressed by the artist's originality, insight, and energy, this series, which included the American premieres of such important features as *Jail Bait*, *Mother Küsters Goes to Heaven*, and *Effi Briest*, proved a revelation beyond our anticipation. Not only was Fassbinder a prodigiously talented, edgy, always surprising filmmaker of acute psychological insight and empathy, but he was also a penetrating social cartographer. He illuminated the ways society circumscribes and influences personal choice: without cynicism and with a natural affection, he made the everyday extraordinary and the bourgeois heroic. Even the films that failed were of enormous interest, sending the viewer's sense of space, rhythm, and dramaturgy whirling.

In 1977 Fassbinder finished his first English-language film, *Despair*, adapted by Tom Stoppard from the novel by Vladimir Nabokov. It was released nationwide in February 1979, and *The Marriage of Maria Braun*, one of the filmmaker's favorite works, was given the honor of closing the New York Film Festival in October 1979. *Maria Braun* was the first in a trilogy Fassbinder wanted to make about the country that formed him, the Germany in which he spent his childhood and adolescence. This was the Germany of the Economic Miracle, presided over by Konrad Adenauer, Chancellor of the Federal Republic. The Adenauer era began in 1949 with a nation in defeat and occupied, its cities in rubble; fourteen years later, Germany had recovered financially, and its citizens were living comfortably, somewhat expansively, and certainly aquisitively. Fassbinder speculated about the moral and psychological price of this breakneck turnaround, and he believed that with it it came forgetfulness. How an individual knew himself was of paramount importance to Fassbinder, and thus the question of personal identity was critical. Identity is formed through engagement with a social whole, and Fassbinder, being German, was eager to explore the notion of German identity. Between the making of *Maria Braun* and his two subsequent narratives of Germany in the 1950s, *Lola* and *Veronika Voss*, Fassbinder completed several other films, including two significant works dealing with earlier periods of modern German history. In 1980 he finished his monumental (fifteen-and-a-half-hour) adaptation for television of Alfred Döblin's 1929 novel *Berlin Alexanderplatz*. In this epic, Franz Biberkopf, an urban Everyman, makes his way through both the 1920s and a distressed society whose idealism is compromised by unemployment, violence, and radical politicians promising order. Through Biberkopf's experiences Fassbinder traces the Weimar Republic lurching toward the Third Reich. *Lili Marleen*, made in 1981, is Fassbinder's only film set in Nazi Germany, and it is one of his most lavish. Made with an international market in mind, its cast was multinational, its narrative pure Hollywood melodrama, and although it was dubbed into German for its American release, it was originally made in English.

The third part of the Adenauer Trilogy, *Veronika Voss*, opened the New York Film Festival in September 1982. In December The Museum of Modern Art hosted the American premiere of *Berlin Alexanderplatz*. The filmmaker, however, could not receive the accolades fast arriving from New York. Fassbinder, who had turned thirty-seven on May 31, died at home in Munich a week and a half later, on the morning of June 10. He left behind an astonishing legacy: forty-three films, produced for cinemas and/or television, made over sixteen-and-a-half years. About a quarter of these, early feature films and works for broadcast television, have not yet been seen in the United States. Of the remaining works, many, like *Despair*, *Veronika Voss*, and *The Marriage of Maria Braun*, have dropped out of distribution since their original release, while others, like *I Only Want You to Love Me*, have only recently become available through Leisure Time Features in New York. So, while it has been possible until now to admire Fassbinder's films individually or in small groupings, this retrospective for the first time allows us to see the work as a whole, to trace, both chronologically and thematically, his development, narrative strategies, and concerns, and to judge each of his films within the context of his entire body of work.

Another factor inhibiting receptiveness to Fassbinder was the media folderol attending his life. He was one of the first internationally celebrated filmmakers who was not embarrassed by being thought of as homosexual. He was often photographed in a leather jacket, defiant and unkempt; this image stood for the man, and this trite representation constantly intruded upon critical judgment of his works. His sudden death, reportedly due to exhaustion and substance abuse, only exaggerated the media's fascination with the ephemera of his naughtiness. When Fassbinder's late works, like *Berlin Alexanderplatz*, *Lola*, *Veronika Voss*, and *Querelle*, appeared in America, their reception vied with the sententious "lesson" of his recent death, but the notion of achievement won out.

Fassbinder's oeuvre is breathtaking. While making films, he continued to direct for the theater and to write stage plays; for other filmmakers he wrote scripts and produced their works. He acted in about forty films. His activity was furious and his art unique. In the fifteen years since his death, his cinema has proven inimitable, but why is not apparent. His films appear effortless, and yet they are virtually impossible to parse. It is astounding that such organicity happened in what is fundamentally a collaborative art form. Part of the answer may be that Fassbinder worked consistently with a team whose members included intimates of the artist. Juliane Lorenz edited all of Fassbinder's films from 1976 to 1982, Kurt Raab was art director from 1969 through 1977, and Peer Raben composed twenty-seven original scores for Fassbinder. Barbara Baum was the costume designer for many of his films, and, when he was not shooting the films himself, he worked primarily with three cameramen: Dietrich Lohmann from 1969 to 1976, Michael Ballhaus from 1970 to 1978, and Xaver Schwarzenberger from 1979 to 1982. The stars of a Fassbinder film were part of an exceptional repertory troupe, and although a performer like Armin Mueller-Stahl in *Lola*, or Günther Lamprecht, in *Berlin Alexanderplatz*, was memorable in the rare Fassbinder film in which each appeared, it is those protean actors and actresses who appeared from film to film, like Harry Baer, Margit Carstensen, Ingrid Caven, Irm Hermann, Hans Hirschmüller, Gottfried John, Gunther Kaufmann, Udo Kier, Ulli Lommel, Klaus Löwitsch, Brigitte Mira, Lilo Pempeit (Liselotte Eder, Fassbinder's mother), Kurt Raab, Hanna Schygulla, Volker Spengler, Barbara Sukowa, and Elisabeth Trissenaar, that give the Fassbinder canon such a satisfying heft. Although troupes are a venerable theatrical tradition, Fassbinder appropriated the idea for the cinema, using it so profoundly and liberally that the notion was both modernized and refreshed.

In the fifteen years since Fassbinder's death, public morality, always a matter of contingency, has caught up with, and in some ways raced beyond, the behavior described in a Fassbinder film. This retrospective therefore will allow viewers for the first time since the films were made to experience each directly and clearly, minus the shock and bewilderment of the new. It will, I believe, be evident that what was radical and original about Fassbinder—a restless and inquiring mind; an ability to unsettle convention, transforming it again and again into something original; a passion for honesty; and a tremendous capacity for beauty—remains so.

Rainer Werner Fassbinder is a two-part endeavor consisting of a complete retrospective of the films and videotapes made by the artist between 1966 and his death in 1982, and this book published by The Museum of Modern Art. The Fassbinder Foundation, Berlin, has been critical to the realization of this project. I join Glenn D. Lowry, Director of the Museum, in expressing the Museum's deep appreciation to Juliane Lorenz, Director of the Fassbinder Foundation, for making this exhibition possible. I am also grateful for her friendship. For their help I thank Annemarie Abel, in the Berlin office, and Ingrid Scheib-Rothbart, the Foundation's representative in New York.

As on the many other occasions in which we have presented German films, Goethe-Institut, New York, has also been a collaborator on this project, and the Department of Film and Video is grateful for the support of its Director, Stephan Nobbe, and Program Coordinator, Brigitte Hubmann.

The Museum of Modern Art is honored that His Excellency, Dr. Jürgen Chrobog, Ambassador of the Federal Republic of Germany, has agreed to serve as patron for this exhibition. Both the Museum and the Fassbinder Foundation thank the following German organizations for their support: Filmboard Berlin-Bradenburg, Potsdam-Babelsberg, and its Director, Prof. Klaus Keil, and the coordinator of the Fassbinder project, Dr. Benedikt Berg-Walz; the Berliner Festspiele GmbH, Berlin; the Embassy of the Federal Republic of Germany, Washington, D.C., and its Cultural Counselor, Gudrun Lücke-Hogaust; the Goethe Institut, Munich, and its President, Hilmar Hoffmann, and the Director of its Film Department, Dr. Bruno Fischli; the Goethe Institute's Washington office, and its Director, Dr. Dieta Sixt; InterNationes, Bonn; the Foreign Ministry of the Federal Republic of Germany (Auswärtiges Amt), Bonn; Export-Union des Deutschen Films e.V., Munich; and Dr. Gunther Witte and Martin Wiebel, Westdeutscher Rundfunk, Cologne. We also acknowledge Filmverlag der Autoren, Munich; the Staatskanzlei Brandenburg, Der Ministerpräsident, Potsdam; and Amanda Mecke, Bantam Doubleday Dell, New York. In addition, we thank the laboratory personnel at Geyer-Werke, Berlin, Hans-Joachim Rabs, Klaus-Peter Schultze, Harald Krause, Gernod Brettmann, and Bernhard Huhn, and at ARRI-Contrast, Berlin, Detlef Fleischhauer and Gerhard Bergfried, for the restorations of *Fear of Fear, Martha,* and *World on a Wire.*

A special note of appreciation goes to Lufthansa and Lufthansa-Cargo, Berlin, for their essential help in shipping the films and travel from Germany to the United States.

Support for this exhibition has also been provided by Christoph Henkel, Düsseldorf; and by the Contemporary Exhibition Fund, established at the Museum with gifts from Lily Auchincloss, Agnes Gund and Daniel Shapiro, and Mr. and Mrs. Ronald S. Lauder. The Department of Film and Video gratefully acknowledges that the Fund makes possible so many of our programs.

We are grateful to the many individuals in Germany, France, and the United States who have contributed to this project, including Alfred Biolek, Cologne; Thomas Dörschel, Berlin; Tim Fischer, Berlin; Dr. Thomas Geyer, Geyer-Werke, Berlin; Peter and Waltraut Green, Munich; Theo Hinz, Munich; Hans Kohl, Taurus Film, Ismaning; Reinhard Penzel, SONY Deutschland GmbH, Cologne; Dr. Günter Rohrbach, Munich; Hanna Schygulla, Paris; Christian Tebert, Berlin; Herbert Volkmann, Berlin; Horst Wendlandt, Rialto-Film, Berlin; and Rosel Zech, Munich.

I extend the warmest thanks to Daniel Talbot and his company, New Yorker Films, the American distributor of many Fassbinder films, for allowing us to prepare this retrospective; and to José Lopez, Vice-President General Manager, for helping the project run so smoothly. I am also grateful to Bruce Pavlow, President of Leisure Time Features, New York, for the loan of several Fassbinder films that Leisure Time releases in the United States.

Although I owe a particular debt to Thomas Elsaesser and Georgia Brown, whose illuminating pieces were written specifically for this publication, I am also indebted to the authors whose works first appeared in the book published by the Foundation in 1992 on the occasion of the tenth anniversary of the filmmaker's death: Harry Baer, Christian Braad Thomsen, Jeanne

Moreau, Hans Helmut Prinzler, Volker Schlöndorff, Wolfram Schütte, Hanna Schygulla, and Wim Wenders. A note of appreciation also goes to the translator of these texts into English, Christa Armstrong; and to Ron Magliozzi, Film Research Assistant, Department of Film and Video, who prepared the filmography.

Working with the Museum's Department of Publications has been rewarding, as always, and I thank Osa Brown, Director; Harriet Schoenholz Bee, Managing Editor; and Cynthia Ehrhardt, Senior Production Assistant. I am also grateful to Jim Hinchee, of Jim Hinchee Design, for the catalogue's attractive and intelligent design, and Jody Hanson, Director, Department of Graphics, for overseeing the design process. My most enthusiastic thanks are reserved for the two excellent editors who brought such insight to this book, Christopher Lyon, who began the project, and Barbara Ross, who completed it.

Many other colleagues at The Museum of Modern Art contributed to this project, and I would like to acknowledge their help: Michael Margitich, Deputy Director for Development; Brett Cobb, Director of Development and Membership; John L. Wielk, Manager, Exhibition and Project Funding; and Meiko Takayama, Manager of Corporate Relations. A special note of thanks goes to Graham Leggat, Film and Video Press Representative, Department of Communications, and, in the Department of Film and Video, Jytte Jensen, Assistant Curator; Mary Corliss, Assistant Curator; Joshua Siegel, Curatorial Assistant; Robert Beers, Executive Assistant; Charles Silver, Film Research Associate; Andrew Haas, Film Expeditor; Pierre Vaz, Film Shipper; Charles Kalinowksi, Head Projectionist; and Anthony Tavolacci, Gregory Singer, and Edward D'Inzillo, Projectionists. I also express my sincerest gratitude to Mary Lea Bandy, Chief Curator, Department of Film and Video, for her unstinting and enthusiastic support of this project.

For her patience and understanding I thank Jillian W. Slonim. Finally, I want to acknowledge Vincent Canby, chief film critic of *The New York Times* from 1969 to 1994, whose sharp insight into Fassbinder helped inform my thinking about the artist, and whose writings on the filmmaker remain fresh and illuminating today.

Laurence Kardish
Curator and Coordinator of Film Exhibitions
The Museum of Modern Art, New York

*Mutter Küsters' Fahrt
zum Himmel (Mother
Küsters Goes to Heaven).*
1975. Ingrid Caven

Martha. 1973.
Margit Carstensen

Wolf Gremm.
Kamikaze 1989.
1981. RWF

A Cinema of Vicious Circles
Thomas Elsaesser

> What I would like is to make Hollywood movies, that is,
> movies as wonderful and universal, but at the same time not as hypocritical, as Hollywood.[1]

Since his death in 1982, Fassbinder's stature as an international auteur undoubtedly has grown, even though the exact nature of his achievement, apart from its profligate prodigality, is far from ascertained. Reassessments of his work have tended to focus on the later films, either around the BRD trilogy, *Berlin Alexanderplatz*, his engagement with the legacy of Nazism, or by re-examining his sexual politics around *Fox and his Friends, In a Year of 13 Moons*, and *Querelle*.[2] In the following, his early films are brought back into view, if only to show how creatively as well as cunningly Fassbinder was able to capitalize on the constraints that ruled his private and professional life.

Like most German directors of his generation, Rainer Werner Fassbinder had to rely on state funding. Except for his first short film, *The City Tramp*, paid for by the male lead, and the two big-budget ventures *Despair* and *Lili Marleen,* his films were made possible by the various forms of public financing available in the Federal Republic in the 1970s and 1980s: project subsidies, television co-production money, the Federal Film Prize, and the so-called *Zusatzfoerderung* (supplementary subsidy). Fassbinder hacking his way through the "subsidy jungle" is a paradox in more than one sense. He made no secret of his contempt for such forms of patronage, boasting (not unfairly) that he could turn in an entire film in the time it took others to read the small print on a grant application form. Shrewd enough to make use of the system, since it provided the necessary liquidity for his rapid turnover and awe-inspiring productivity, Fassbinder remained keenly aware that the state actually paid the filmmaker to be a nonconformist. In an ambiguous relation between authority and rebellion, the filmmaker bit the hand that fed him while the state condemned the artist to play the licensed clown and professional enfant terrible.

Not every director of the New German Cinema saw as clearly as Fassbinder the irony of being a kept filmmaker—kept in order to be critical. When Fassbinder was asked to account for his success, at the time when *Why Does Herr R. Run Amok?* was released in 1969, he replied: "The established culture business needs outsiders like me."[3] The mutual dependence of a liberal democracy and its critics was staged in West Germany for the most part as a case of mistaken integrity, with both sides earnestly insisting on creative independence, while more objective commentators talked about the "new Caligaris."[4] Yet for Fassbinder, this relationship was just one more example of what could be called his "cinema of vicious circles," where the dynamics of power and complicity, of impossible choices, of honest bad faith and unenviable alternatives play across the whole social field, from filmmaking to lovemaking, from deals with international producers to deals with Munich drug pushers. Fassbinder seems to have been energized by these vicious circles, since he relished and cultivated them throughout his career: if in the early films they underpin his plots without necessarily becoming the explicit theme, the later films make them their outer, political horizon until, in *The Third Generation*, released in 1978, collusion between authority and rebellion furnishes the film's very subject matter, as terrorists are paid by the state in order to justify its law-and-order policies. The notion of vicious circles also helps make sense of Fassbinder's ambition to direct Hollywood movies, but "not as hypocritical." Whether in the key of Sirkean melodrama, or blown up to UFA-style bombast, whether art cinema chamber piece, self-revealing docudrama, or satirical send-up of his own louche demimonde, his films all have at their center the hard core of a contradiction, an unsentimental, detachedly lucid point where the plot lines cross to motivate a moral or emotional impasse, sensed by the characters and recognized by the viewer.

It may seem that Fassbinder was making obvious choices in devoting his early films to the gangster genre and the clichés of film noir, but those choices were also determined by the kinds of emotion he wanted to evoke, and by the sensations he remembered from his adolescent moviegoing. Reflecting a then-fashionable existential angst, his various nostalgias were kept in check by an intelligence able to devise dramatic deadlocks. Even the later melodramas of idealism and renunciation, such as *Effi Briest* and *The Marriage of Maria Braun*, which proved as popular in the 1980s as such women's pictures had been decades earlier, have the toughness of fables that bolt tight all exits for the characters.

What set Fassbinder apart from other German filmmakers most decisively was his conviction that in order to be a Hollywood director in Germany, he had to organize his own production base and make it function like the American studio system, even if he had to reinvent each of its interlocking mechanisms. Rejecting the image of the solitary artist crafting his work, Fassbinder "industrialized" and "incorporated" filmmaking. And, ironically, the ideas of teamwork and collective decisionmaking, which had wide appeal in the 1970s, permitted him to build up his own kind of hierarchy. If not exactly the Hollywood system's division of labor, Fassbinder's stick-and-carrot methods still facilitated fast work, with a minimum of instructions or explanations, though he also thereby held his collaborators, as they often enough claimed after his death, in the vice grip of emotional blackmail.[5]

That these supposedly biographical dynamics are reflected in the films is one of the most frequent themes in writing about Fassbinder, but it is important to recognize in his work a more conceptual preoccupation with what it means to make films intended for a mainstream public: "The American method of making [films] left the audience with emotions and nothing else," he explained. "I want to give the spectator the emotions along with the possibility of reflecting on and analyzing what he is feeling."[6]

In the early films, "reflecting on" the feelings of the characters often took the form of avoiding even the suspicion of emotion. *Love Is Colder than Death*, for example, displays such emotional detachment and understatement that a contemporary reviewer complained, "the film comes out of an almost unimaginable fear that an emotion might occur which the director wouldn't wish to answer for."[7] The desires binding people to each other in these films are those common to all popular culture: love and money. But these twin strands of action and feeling are braided together and twisted into a shape that makes their inextricability axiomatic, and therefore not so much a moral stance as a formal structure. If we look at the plots of Fassbinder's first five films, it becomes apparent that they describe a similar configuration, which could be schematized as: A wants x, but needs B to get it. B wants y, which can only be had with the help of A. The structure could be one of perfect symmetry or even exchange: B gives x to A, who makes sure B gets y. But the situation is complicated by two factors: firstly, there are usually also C and D, whose function it is to block access to x or y or both; but even where there is neither C nor D to impede the exchange, x and y are incommensurate, not of the same order of being, in precisely the way that love and money are incommensurate. To put it differently: both A and B undervalue what the other wants and overvalue what they want from the other.

All the films state these inversely symmetrical relations bluntly and blandly. In *Love Is Colder than Death*, Franz wants Bruno, but can only get him by standing in for him. Johanna wants Franz, which is why she wants to eliminate Bruno. But targeting Bruno means hitting Franz. Bruno tries to eliminate Johanna, but is himself eliminated instead. Johanna gets Franz, but has by then lost him to Bruno. In *Gods of the Plague*, Margarethe wants Franz, but Franz wants Günther. Günther no longer wants Johanna, who still wants Franz. Günther has killed Franz's brother; Johanna causes Franz to get killed. Only Margarethe and Johanna survive, bound together but also separated by having lost Franz. At the end of *Whity*, the actors who play Günther (now Whity) and Johanna (now Hanna) are also the only ones who escape, but merely in order to perish. Günther returns as Ricky in *The American Soldier*, still wanted by Franz. But Ricky, like Bruno, is paid by the policemen looking for Ricky, who is an object of value because he loves nobody, not even Rosa, who loves him, and whom he kills when told to do so. Margarethe kills herself, when she is no longer wanted by her lover, so that both Rosa and Margarethe foretell the fate of Franz's love for Ricky, who is the cause of Franz getting killed in the final showdown. In *The Niklashausen Journey*, the lay preacher wants to be a saint, for which he needs the black monk. The black monk wants a social uprising, for which he needs money. The countess does not need her money and gives it to the monk, but wants the preacher for his body. . . .

No doubt this structural configuration could be further refined, but with only minor permutations it fits most of Fassbinder's subsequent films as well: a matrix as aesthetically satisfying as it is emotionally frustrating. Yet another "vicious circle," it draws attention to the fact that Fassbinder repeats on the textual level what has already been identified on the production level: ordered to bite the hand that feeds him, he elaborates for his heroes allegories of freedom and dependency. But there is another moral position implied in such a formal structure. To call it a vicious circle is to argue that a fundamental insufficiency and imbalance emerge from the pattern, which are often ironically underscored, inviting two complementary, if contradictory, responses from the spectator.

One response is resignation to the inevitability of there being only losers in these emotional barters. This is especially true of a later film such as *In a Year of 13 Moons*, where Erwin/Elvira's relentless slide to suicide is the consequence of meticulously and mercilessly chronicled acts of failed exchange. But it also applies to *The Bitter Tears of Petra von Kant*, *Mother Küsters Goes to Heaven*, and *Fox and His Friends*, because in each case a gap opens up between what is given and what is received, whether it be love, trust, or money. The other response is to see the films tracing these patterns, and repeating them, in order to retrace

the contours of a circularity, as if animated by the desperate and indefatigable hope of nevertheless finding a way out at the weakest point. Such would be the utopian perspective that the films have to offer, and much of the feel and impact of Fassbinder's early films—an insistently self-lacerating pessimism shot through with moments of ecstatic (and, in the event, gratuitous) optimism, as during the first meeting between "the Gorilla" and Franz in *Gods of the Plague*—seems to come from the need to discover a liberating dialectic inside a situation emotionally experienced as inescapable, closed, self-perpetuating. Such at least is one of the meanings of the phrase from *Beware of a Holy Whore*: "The only feeling I can accept is despair."

What actually makes the early films different from the melodramas is not the central preoccupation, which remains the same throughout the decade, but rather the fact that Fassbinder's films have a double perspective on these vicious circles: from without and from within. All his films are about couples, but the films up to and including *Beware of a Holy Whore* have in common that the couple relationships are seen either in the context of other couples or of the group: the perspective "from without" is the group's view of the couple, which thus also reflects the collectivist, antifamily ideology that Fassbinder professed to share with the rest of his generation. From *The Merchant of Four Seasons* onward, however, the emphasis shifts, and the couple is seen more from within, often from the vantage point of the weaker partner.

In *Merchant* Fassbinder persuades us that we are seeing certain crucial scenes from the protagonist Hans's viewpoint, even though he is not actually present. This applies to the cheerless and hysterical lovemaking between his wife and a man she casually allows to pick her up in the street (the logic of which demands that Hans neither be present nor know about it). Wilhelm Roth has quite aptly described the effect at which Fassbinder is aiming: "In the scenes where [Hans] is absent, the characters behave as he would imagine them behaving, or as he fears, knows, or anticipates them behaving, as they have to behave, because reacting to his reaction, which in turn is his response to their reaction, etc. Against this vicious circle, from which at first he wants to escape (he is the first Fassbinder protagonist who not only succeeds in getting away—this is true also of *Rio das Mortes*—but who also returns, disillusioned), he ends up not putting up any resistance. The way he gradually falls silent [is] an even stronger accusation than would be the loudest outcry."[8] Even more startlingly paradoxical is Hans's funeral, shot as if he were observing the mourners. This seems to gratify a common childhood fantasy, namely to see how sorry people are when you are dead and how much they regret having been so horrid, but with the added twist that the mourners at his funeral, with one exception, are not sorry but relieved. It is intimated throughout the film that Hans is already "beyond the grave," and that he has, in a sense, been cheated also of his second death, the symbolic one of memory and destiny, and it is this, which he has sensed all along, that drives him to suicide.

The motor of Fassbinder's productivity is what he himself called "emotional exploitation." All his films, when seen "from without," are ingeniously dramatized and occasionally didactic statements about what it means to have power over someone else's capacity for love and thus to live within mutual dependencies structured around generosity and guilt: "Every decent director has only one subject, and finally only makes the same film over and over again. My subject is the exploitability of feelings, whoever might be the one exploiting them. It never ends. It's a permanent theme. Whether the state exploits patriotism, or whether in a couple relationship, one partner destroys the other." It is when examining the subtler but also more devastating dynamics of exploitation among couples that the vantage point "from without" eventually gives way to the perspective "from within."

Determined to prove, with varying degrees of conviction, that his heroes' personal predicaments have a wider social significance, Fassbinder became more overtly political without, however, allowing his characters insights into possible escape routes from the vicious circles that bind them to each other in emotional blackmail or exploitation, and he showed remarkable inventiveness in devising stories that demonstrated this process in action. Graphic portrayals of the predicament across different social worlds and different human situations earned him a reputation as a chronicler of postwar German mores, personal vicissitudes, and social inequalities; but the very same obstinacy of sticking to his chosen theme was also responsible for the more negative judgment of Fassbinder as a politically naive polemicist with a rather narrow range of social insights.

> What I can always claim about myself and my films: even the so-called little
> people are allowed to have big feelings.[9]

In Fassbinder's films, stylized behavior against an artless or even seedy backdrop draws attention to a basic inadequacy: the physical and verbal gestures of the protagonists never match their intentions, and an irrecoverable but spellbinding ambivalence surrounds their own role-playing. In *Gods of the Plague* or *Recruits in Ingolstadt*, for instance, the viewer is invited to identify with the characters, but also to laugh at them, to recognize their psychological situations and moral conflicts and yet be disconcerted by their self-convinced theatricality. None of the customary attitudes of identification (whether the distancing of comedy or the involvement of drama or suspense) sits comfortably on the films. This unsettling, dephasing element could be seen as Fassbinder's debt to Bertolt Brecht, making a queasy feeling between stifled laughter and embarrassed empathy the filmic equivalent of the "alienation effect." Yet amid the beautifully executed camera movements, the classically balanced shots, and the languid pans, another rupture is also present. The shabbiness of the decor and the tinsel

Faustrecht der Freiheit
(Fox and His Friends).
1974. Karlheinz Böhm

glamour of the actresses, their comic and touching incongruity, manage to convey the sense that the film one is watching is the melancholy echo of an ideal world yet to be shamed into existence. The gap between ambition and achievement, which such inadequacy implies, has a double edge: its "failure" the promise of perfection forever deferred, it nonetheless locates the king-size dreams of the characters—defiantly asserted against an unresponsive environment—as fond illusions, fated to fizzle out ignominiously. The films thus reflect a twofold frustration: an imagination already secondhand is further foiled at the level of performance, and Fassbinder shows himself a realist with critical intentions precisely insofar as his films are documentary records of what one might call an outcast's starvation fantasies.

For this reason, perhaps, no unified emotional perspective was either possible or desirable. In *Gods of the Plague* the strategy works especially well: "Fassbinder reduces the action to a minimum, he freeze-dries his dialogues like Hemingway, and then defrosts them again thanks to a very gentle and melancholy poetry."[10] This "gentle and melancholy poetry" was to become the tenor of Fassbinder's subsequent films. Voyeuristic projection is no longer disguised by being motivated through identification with a character inside a coherent, autonomous fictional universe, but emerges nakedly and disjointedly as the uneasy perception of the film as a performance, as the exaggerated gesture of self-conscious make-believe, not unlike the performances in a pornographic movie: the spectator begins to worry whether the actors themselves can keep up the pretence. This discrepancy, forced to the point of physical discomfort in films like *The American Soldier* and *Whity*, but equally present in *Ali: Fear Eats the Soul* and *Fox and His Friends*, also has its poetry: that of images and gestures precariously balanced between awkwardness and beauty, between reticence and self-display. In the dialectic of false images and real feelings, such poetry lends itself to a Godardian reflection about the cinema itself, its manipulative images and the rhetoric of its effects; it also represents a provisional formulation of Fassbinder's moral theme, for he makes palpable—whether deliberately or by default—the sometimes terrifying and grotesque distance between the subjective mise-en-scène of the characters and the objective mise-en-scène of the camera, between the way the characters perceive themselves and the way others (notably the viewer) perceive them: "I'm against caricatures, I'm against parodies . . . if you say that this scene [in *The American Soldier*, when the chambermaid commits suicide] has the effect of a parody, then I have to take your word for it, but then I'm ashamed of myself and I apologize."[11] Thus, even where a character's pretensions might disavow themselves by their own lack of verisimilitude, her gestures are nonetheless taken seriously, in order to allow the audience a space.

In the example from *The American Soldier* just quoted, Margarethe von Trotta slowly plunges a kitchen knife into her abdomen when her lover tells her over the phone that their affair is over. This may seem a parody to some viewers, but it lingers on as one of the most memorable and mysterious moments of the film, something like its secret center. At other times, the sheer improbability of a character's self-image is shown to exert irresistible fascination over others, to the extent that it can be traded in for power that causes real harm and hurt: in the same film, Ricky, a Vietnam veteran turned hired killer, is in a sense wholly pre-posterous. But given that the characters in the film are devoid of gestures or a language to call their own and gladly accept the world of a gangster film as "real" because of its uncomplicated coherence, their willingness to act even the parts of victims in this borrowed world becomes less implausible. What registers is the absurd but moving idealism of someone trying to emulate small-time crooks and supermarket thieves. The films are ultimately compelling precisely because of a precarious balancing act between characters pretending to be casual and our perception of the effort it takes them to appear so. What seems comic or parodic is the terrifying iron grip alienation seems to have on the gestures and the bodies, as the invisible social machinery of conformism, peer-group pressure, and romantic cliché force their lives under the cookie-cutter of destiny.

However, the more Fassbinder came to trust his ability to walk the fine line between bathos and pathos, parody and sincerity—in other words, the more securely he could portray the authentic representation of inauthentic roles—the more the gangster genre must have seemed an impasse, especially in expressing the broken and unresolved relationship that a middle-class filmmaker maintains with the proletarian residue in the society around him, which in Fassbinder's case had to do with the unashamed emotionalism, liberating vulgarity, and direct sexuality of the kind of popular culture found in Munich, a city at once provincial-Bavarian and urban-international.

If *The Merchant of Four Seasons* can be called Fassbinder's first film with a definitely proletarian hero, it is due less to the realism of the Munich setting or the ordinariness of the char-acter of Hans Epp, than to the fact that his emotions are registered along a single dramatic and stylistic continuum—still on the razor's edge, maybe, between sentimental tragedy and *Wirtschaftswunder* kitsch, but with no ambivalence surrounding the character's role-playing, and without viewers having the uneasy sense that they are watching a documentary about figures playing out self-created fictions. Instrumental in this change of attitude to the characters was Fassbinder's discovery of the films of Douglas Sirk, the German émigré director who made a string of popular films at Universal in the 1950s, often starring matinee idols like Rock Hudson and John Derek, for producer Ross Hunter, a specialist in women's films and technicolor weepies. Fassbinder's discovery—documented in an essay he wrote in 1971 on six Sirk films he had just seen—proved momentous: it rehabilitated a then–almost-forgotten director and renewed interest in a genre that was to gain considerable critical prominence in subsequent years: the Hollywood family melodrama.[12]

The Merchant of Four Seasons is remarkable in showing a lower-middle-class charac-ter actually wanting to become working-class, and it gives this class the kind of inwardness and subjectivity that the nineteenth-century novel reserved for the tribulations of the bourgeoisie, and that the Hollywood films of Nicholas Ray, Otto Preminger, Vincente Minnelli, or Joseph Losey locate in middle America. In their films, every character is justified within his own terms; there are no outright villains, only victims, sometimes of society, but just as often of themselves. A character like James Mason's megalomaniac father in Ray's *Bigger than Life*, the ex-GI played by Frank Sinatra in Minnelli's *Some Came Running*, or the corrupt policemen in Preminger's *Where the Sidewalk Ends* and Losey's *The Prowler*, are figures that can also be found in the Fassbinder films of the mid-1970s. In *The Merchant of Four Seasons*, *Jail Bait*, *Ali: Fear Eats the Soul*, *Martha*, *The Bitter Tears of Petra von Kant*, *Fox and his Friends*, and *Fear of Fear*, the moral or emotional constellation of characters appears to be held together by a kind of master narrative in which a parent, spouse, or friend either makes sadistic demands on the hero or heroine (*Merchant*, *Martha*, *Petra von Kant*, *Fox*) or betrays, deceives, or abandons him or her (*Jail Bait*, *Ali: Fear Eats the Soul*, *Fox*, *Fear of Fear*). The dilemma is again one of

*Händler der vier
Jahreszeiten (The Merchant
of Four Seasons).* 1971.
Irm Hermann

insufficiency, of not measuring up to external demands, but for the audience, the drama arises at precisely the point where we become aware that the dominating figures in the relationship—any possibility of resolution having been carefully eliminated—also have their reasons, and indeed are either well-meaning, as in *Jail Bait* and *Fear of Fear*, or themselves vulnerable and boxed in, as in *Petra von Kant*, *Fox*, *Ali: Fear Eats the Soul*, or *Effi Briest*.

The strength of the Hollywood tradition he adopted, whether one thinks of it as the family melodrama of the 1950s (*Ali: Fear Eats the Soul*, *Bolwieser*), or the "women's picture" of the 1940s (*Petra von Kant*, *Martha*, *Effi Briest*, *The Marriage of Maria Braun*, *Lola*, *Veronica Voss*), is that its emphasis on negative subjectivity—love unrequited, hopes dashed, agonized waiting, painful embarrassment, tragic misunderstandings, trust betrayed, terrifying self-doubt, and suspicion—already indicates the extent to which, even in mainstream cinema, subjectivity is necessarily a negativity, a mere effect or trace of an irreconcilable split for which the vicious circles designate at once the "ground" and the "figure." Fassbinder's adoption of Sirkean melodrama thus becomes especially comprehensible when the genre is seen under the aspect that made it most suspect: its inauthenticity. Once again, this is the view "from without," whereas "from within," domestic melodrama connotes most forcefully the presence of a desiring subject in the discourse, figured as both cause and effect, the reason why the protagonist must come to grief, his failure in the world being at the same time his most intense self-affirmation. In retrospect, it is clear that what made Sirk such an overdetermined choice for Fassbinder was that his films combine extremes of stylization and visual excess with a nearly Greek form of tragic inevitability, while Sirk also achieved, in films that subtly but devastatingly exposed the hypocrisy of middle-class American morality, another ideal Fassbinder strove for: Hollywood movies, but not as hypocritical.

Dorothy Malone, the sister [of Robert Stack, in Written on the Wind*] is the only one who is in love with the right person, i.e., Rock Hudson, and she stands by her love, which is ridiculous, of course. It has to be ridiculous when everyone else thinks their surrogate actions are the real thing, it is quite clear that everything she does, she does because she can't have the real thing. . . . Dorothy does something bad, she sets her brother against Lauren [Bacall] and Rock. All the same, I love her as I rarely love anyone in the cinema, as a spectator I follow with Douglas Sirk the traces of human despair. In* Written on the Wind *the good, the "normal," the "beautiful" are always utterly revolting; the evil, the weak, the dissolute arouse one's compassion.* [13]

It is not difficult to recognize in this description the plot lines of many of Fassbinder's own films, a variation of the blueprint or master narrative already mentioned. Similarly, Sirk's life and work were exemplary for Fassbinder, not least as symbolizing a precious continuity between Hollywood films and the German popular cinema. An acknowledged master of both, Sirk belongs to the "good Germany" of Weimar; he was a man of the theater who made the move into film and, despite being an intellectual, had no contempt for the popular. If Sirk's biography thus makes him the perfect elective father for the fatherless Fassbinder, the bond was strengthened by the fact that Fassbinder was retracing in reverse the trajectory of Sirk: the latter traveled from the Berlin UFA style to that of Universal, while Fassbinder's journey was from homemade Hollywood director to one of the stars of Bavaria Studio at Geiselgasteig, itself the heir after 1945 to UFA-Neubabelsberg, and the site where Fassbinder shot some of the biggest productions of the postwar German cinema, *Berlin Alexanderplatz* and *Lili Marleen.*

There had not been a talent since Bertolt Brecht in the 1920s so distinctive in voice and signature, nor one so adept at playing with and exploiting the media to gain access to the market. Perhaps he could hardly have done otherwise, since, for better or for worse, Fassbinder seemed condemned to overproduce in order to produce at all, and in this sense he was a filmmaker whose working methods reflected the objective conditions of a capitalist mode of production, albeit one in its premonopolistic, competitive phase. As such, he may well have been the most flamboyantly flowering hothouse plant the curiously underdeveloped and artificially backward German film industry produced after the war, obliged to repeat (in part) the development of Hollywood, but historically out of phase.

The films were autobiographical in a very straightforward manner: they translated into fictional terms and formal configurations the personal experience of filmmaking. Having to overproduce in order to produce at all suggests the vicious circle of capitalist logic. Having to sell himself as an independent producer to those with money, the state, the press, and the public, while at the same time having to manipulate and exploit others to extract from them their loyalty and labor: may this not be another vicious circle where the victim cannot escape being oppressive, and the oppressor is himself the victim? A capitalist entrepreneur in an age of monopolies, Fassbinder wanted to articulate a vision of utopian liberation and protean self-creation, while being himself in chains. The vicious circles, which seem closed at first, opened up in rather unsuspected ways—towards the economic "spinning top" of the subsidy system. The harder Fassbinder pushed and the faster he turned, the more money seemed available to him, provided he converted it into yet another film. It was as if only the acceleration of the circuits of exchange could break the vicious circles of his life and work, as if the instability of the system were what ultimately made it so efficient and also so murderous.

Fassbinder's ambition to make Hollywood films in Germany was only partly realized in the years between 1975 and 1982. On the one hand, his furious production schedules set a pace that neither his fellow directors of the state-funded New German Cinema nor the moribund commercial film industry could hope to follow. His energy and charisma put him in command of a working method—a ministudio with superstars, a regular team, and a familiar cast of character actors—which might have professionalized filmmaking in Germany, had it not been perceived as such a mocking critique of the cultural bureaucracies, the "cinema by committee" on which almost every other German filmmaker in the 1970s and 1980s depended. On the other hand, his films—even box office successes like *The Marriage of Maria Braun*— never quite escaped the elitist connotations of an author's cinema, either at home or abroad. At home, it was *Effi Briest*, the tasteful adaptation of a well-loved classic of nineteenth-century German literature, that brought him widest recognition before *The Marriage of Maria Braun* and *Lili Marleen* once more fanned the flames of both fame and notoriety, while never quite granting him the love a national audience reserves for its favorite femmes fatales or male comedy stars. As Andrew Sarris once remarked, Fassbinder's fate was to belong to a country where the cinema knew "no middle ground between the mandarins and the masses."[14] New York, the city that gave him in 1975 the retrospective that confirmed him as "the greatest talent in Europe," might well be the place where, some two decades later, Fassbinder and his films finally transcend both the mandarins and the masses, to become what the cinema has to offer by way of universality: a classic.

A previous version of this essay was published in 1976.

1. Interview with Rainer Werner Fassbinder by Wilfried Wiegand, in Peter W. Jansen and Wolfram Schütte, eds., *Rainer Werner Fassbinder* (Frankfurt: Fischer, 1992), pp. 93–94.
2. See the author's "Fassbinder: Historicising the Subject: A Body of Work?," in *New German Critique*, no. 63 (Fall 1994), pp. 11–34.
3. Quoted in *Frankfurter Allgemeine Zeitung* 6 (July 1970). The irony did not escape *New York Times* film critic Vincent Canby either: "There is little ambiguity about what the director is up to here. *Katzelmacher* is scathing about the postwar economic boom that has, of course, been so kind to the filmmaker himself" ("Katzelmacher Hypnotizes and Amuses, *The New York Times*, June 4, 1977); "*Why Does Herr R. Run Amok* is full of sneers for the same German affluence that has made Mr. Fassbinder's extraordinary film career possible, but that's the way with many artists these days. They must bite the hands as long as they feed them" ("Fassbinder Sneers at German Affluence," *The New York Times*, November 18, 1977).
4. Joerg Friedrich Krabbe, "Die neuen Caligaris," *Neues Forum* (Vienna), July/August 1976, pp. 59–64.
5. See H. G. Pflaum/R. W. Fassbinder, *Das bißchen Realität das ich brauche* (Munich: Hanser, 1976), where Pflaum is the participant-observer on the sets of *Satan's Brew* and *Chinese Roulette*.
6. "I Let the Audience Feel and Think," interview with Rainer Werner Fassbinder by Norbert Sparrow, *Cineaste* 8, no. 2 (Fall 1977), p. 20.
7. "Chronik und Bilanz des Internationalen Films," *Film*, no. 12 (1969), p. 65.
8. Wilhelm Roth, "Kommentierte Filmographie," in Jansen and Schütte, eds., *Rainer Werner Fassbinder*, p. 151.
9. Quoted in Marion Schmid and Herbert Gehr, eds., *Werkschau Katalog* (Berlin: Argon, 1992), p. 224.
10. Michael Lenz, *Westdeutsche Allgemeine Zeitung*, July 31, 1970.
11. Interview with Wilfried Wiegand, in Jansen and Schütte, eds., *Rainer Werner Fassbinder*, p. 84.
12. "Six Films by Douglas Sirk," in Laura Mulvey and Jon Halliday, eds., *Douglas Sirk* (Edinburgh Festival, 1971), pp. 95–107. In the wake of the Sirk revival, melodrama was to undergo a fairly radical reëvaluation in the 1970s and 1980s, partly escaping the blanket condemnation of Hollywood as the purveyor of reactionary ideology, and partly because of the interest shown by feminist film theory in "women's pictures." See Christine Gledhill, ed., *Home Is Where the Heart Is* (London: British Film Institute, 1986).
13. "Six Films by Douglas Sirk," pp. 98, 100.
14. "The basic problem with German cinema is that there is no middle ground between the mandarins and the masses, between the festival places and the grind houses. . . . Fassbinder, I think, can provide pleasure even for the ordinary moviegoer dwelling within the older boundaries of life. Fassbinder deftly balances style (Straub) with humanity (Herzog) in such a way that *The Merchant of Four Seasons* manages to break the heart without betraying the mind" (Andrew Sarris, "Lost Love, Found Despair," *The Village Voice*, November 22, 1973).

Lili Marleen. 1980.
RWF, Hanna Schygulla

Die Ehe der Maria Braun (The Marriage of Maria Braun). 1978. *Trümmerfrauen* ("rubble women") in a scene set in Berlin, 1945

"A Very Sad Song Sung with Lots of Feeling"
Georgia Brown

I'm grateful to Fassbinder for putting his personal pain on screen again and again. In his naked, no-exit narratives, the closeness of adult unhappiness to childhood trauma, of monstrousness to helplessness, is clear and emphatic. Endless cycles of (child) longing and (adult) betrayal are enacted, most of these ending in suicide, murder, fatal accident, or the deadliest compromise, suicide of the spirit. Only twice, in two late Hanna Schygulla vehicles, *The Marriage of Maria Braun* and *Lili Marleen*, does the pattern crack significantly and the central character break free into something like an outward "I want to live!" spiral. Because escape can be more intolerable than death, she's technically defeated at the end, although defeat does not invalidate her glorious triumph.

In a slow business like show business, no one has worked at Fassbinder's compulsive pace—thirty-five full-length films, including the thirteen-part *Berlin Alexanderplatz*, not to mention the television productions and plays. Schygulla asks the obvious question, "Did he die so young because he was in such a rush, or did he rush so because he was destined to die young?" (After the fact, one can read premonitions of early death everywhere in the films.) But another reason for rushing may have been that interludes between films left him in an intolerable depressive limbo.

If the films were as melancholy as the narratives alone suggest, they would be impossible to bear—for the director, I suspect, as well as the viewer. What buoys them, makes them exhilarating, is the lightness of kitsch—Fassbinder's pushing or tweaking sentiment toward comedy—as well as the inestimable consolation of what Julia Kristeva called (in *Black Sun*), "Beauty: depression's other realm." A bereft child (barely acknowledged by his father, alternately neglected and overstimulated by his mother), Fassbinder was educated and consoled by the movies and knew what it is that compulsive moviegoers crave: to have their terrible loneliness alleviated, to be vindicated, and to be stirred to the roots by irresistible beauty.

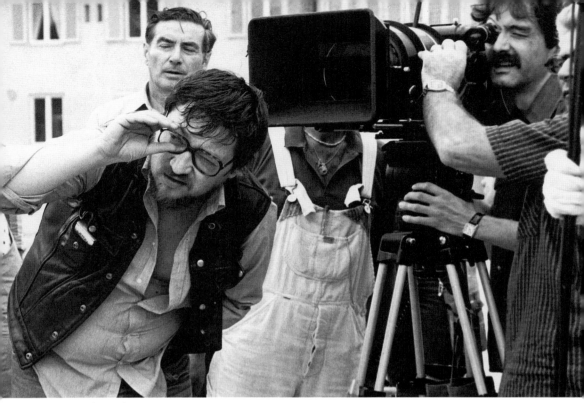

RWF, Xaver Schwarzenberger
(behind camera) on the set
of *Lili Marleen*, 1980

It took him a long time to create heroes who weren't beaten down. In most Fassbinder films, holy innocents are scorned, mocked as ugly, and eventually forced by the "normal" outside world to eliminate themselves. Dependency makes them weak, weakness makes them prey. In the wonderfully sad and funny scene in *Why Does Herr R. Run Amok?* where the pudgy, oblivious Herr R. (Kurt Raab) stops at a music store to buy a record, he becomes the butt of a joke that the audience is in on but also sees beyond. He's trying to appease his unappeasable wife (read, "parent") by finding a song to make her happy. It's "a very sad song sung with lots of feeling," he earnestly tells the salesgirls, who can barely stifle their giggles—especially when he goes on to hum the tune. A great deal of comedy is based on pathos, but usually the pathos is hidden away.

"A very sad song sung with lots of feeling": it's a phrase that describes the films themselves. The feeling and grace that the song is sung with can make pain bearable, transform despair into voluptuous melancholy. The way a torch singer uses her voice, Fassbinder uses the camera.

The Merchant of Four Seasons begins typically for a Fassbinder film, with a nasty rejection, although it's hard to imagine a rejection more brutal or more primal. Hans Epp comes back from the Foreign Legion, only to be greeted by his mother's wish that he had died. A "good-for-nothing," she calls him; he should have been killed, she says, instead of her friend's nice boy. Immediately juxtaposed with this scene is a beautiful, uplifting (or upward-lifting) one, combining a barrow filled with green pears, an empty courtyard's austere stonework, and Hans's beseeching, upturned face as he turns round and round, circling and calling out his plaintive, placating song: "Fresh pears, lovely pears. . . ." In the corner, concealed under a doorway, his severe, disapproving wife (she's taken the mother's place) adjusts her garter (seductiveness that frustrates), while high up in a white, gauzy window waits the inviting but unattainable princess.

As Hans turns round and round, and the camera records his dizzying euphoria, he's like a child performing some private ecstatic rite. There's a religious aura: supplication becomes prayer.

Fassbinder often opens with some version of this longing/rejection scenario. Usually a tantalizing beauty and a blossoming of desire are followed by an act of cruelty. And often Fassbinder uses circling to represent bliss. His affinity for spiral staircases may have to do not only with the bannisters' pattern but with the circling required to go up or down. In *Effi Briest*, there's the uplift of Effi's joyful swinging—soon to be stifled.

The Stationmaster's Wife, an excruciating portrait of a marriage (it's *Madame Bovary* from Charles's as well as Emma's point of view), opens onto the newlyweds' frozen embrace, a blurred composition with the otherworldly feel of an Edvard Munch painting. When Bolwieser mounts his bride after their kiss, she pushes him off. Immediately following is a beautiful, lingering pan of shimmering white satin and lace (the discarded bridal gown). Hanni's beauty stimulates her childish husband's neediness—a neediness almost too primitive to bear. At one point, we see him excitedly steaming a windowpane with his breath in order to draw a crude female figure.

As in *The Merchant of Four Seasons*, the longing/rejection pattern is quickly repeated twice. The second time, the embracing pair spins passionately; ardor is quenched by Hanni again pushing Bolwieser away. A short while later, however, the ecstatic swirl is repeated when Hanni waltzes with the handsome butcher, Merkl; there's no rejection. Hanni soon pays a visit to Merkl's immaculate white-tiled shop, where the two retreat to the back room, presumably to make love among the carcasses. For Bolwieser, Hanni's betrayal is a sort of butchery or emasculation. Even more than Hans Epp, Bolwieser is progressively infantilized—at one point he slips his thumb in his mouth—and by the end he's reduced to complete, abject dependence. (This said, what's powerful about *The Stationmaster's Wife* is that Hanni is not demonized. The movie also recognizes her terrible plight, her confused response to the realization that she has married an incorrigibly infantile man.)

A connection between betrayal and emasculation is nowhere so explicit as in the anguished *In a Year of 13 Moons*, where Elvira (formerly Erwin) has had a sex-change operation and suffers the mutilation. The film begins with a lovely idyll, a peaceful trysting spot by a river at dusk. A man picks up Elvira (whom he believes to be a transvestite) and gropes her beautiful white satin (bridal?) underwear, only to discover that he's a she, whereupon he beats her up. Bruised and bloody, Elvira staggers home, where she's only to be rejected again—humiliated and literally dumped (off the hood of his car)—by her live-in lover, Christoph. In *The Stationmaster's Wife* there's a visit to the butcher's shop, but here Fassbinder insists on a tour of a slaughterhouse, an assaultive, agonizing, yet ecstatic scene, with Elvira mimicking Christoph's distraught, intoxicating lines ("And though a man is silenced by his pain, God gave me the power to say how much I suffer"), words competing with barely watchable images.

Tension between beauty and cruelty must have been something Fassbinder required for his own sake, something remembered, something that gave him solace. In *The Stationmaster's Wife*, the cruel Hanni is consistently presented in terms of rhetorical beauty, even when she behaves most coldly. Towards the end, when she sneaks away to meet her oily hairdresser on a train, the sordid assignation is photographed tenderly, lyrically, as if we were watching a great passion. Hanni's beauty underlines her husband's pathos. Bolwieser confuses his desire for his wife with her desire for other men. In a sense, he has become her.

In *The Marriage of Maria Braun* and *Lili Marleen*, beauty, the ecstatic, takes over and drives the narrative. But now beauty is at one with good and the innocent is no longer the victim. Corrosive rejection comes only at the end, and then it is too late to make a difference in the film's momentum (or to dint the viewer's enthusiasm). *Maria Braun* and *Lili Marleen* are usually talked

Lili Marleen. 1980.
Hanna Schygulla

of as problem films and rationalized politically, in terms of fascism, the German economic miracle, and so forth. I think that Fassbinder was content with these readings—indeed, he provided the fuel for them—because he was unsure of himself working in a new "naive" way. These two films are as close as Fassbinder came to making the "naive," Hollywood-style film that he envied.[1]

    Maria Braun begins with an interrupted marriage. But in contrast to *The Stationmaster's Wife*, the newlyweds are separated by fate and love, and mutual longing (rather than repulsion) continues to be the film's driving force. Although I take the baby's cry heard above the sirens and bombs to represent Fassbinder's 1945 birth, I don't, as some do, regard the film as being about his parents' generation but as that baby's fight to live, albeit separate from what it loves and wants to be reunited with. Even though Fassbinder kills off Maria, his comic merging of suburban apocalypse with Germany's soccer triumph ("Deutschland ist Weltmeister!") feels like unquenchable euphoria—the director crowing over his own liberation from the depressive narrative.

    Parenthetically, the script's original ending—Maria drives a car, with Hermann in it, over a precipice—would seem indebted to *Jules and Jim*, another film about a free-spirited woman fighting a conspiracy between the two men who love her. In *Maria Braun's* final scenes, Fassbinder also refers to Godard's *Contempt*—having Hermann, while Maria dresses, pace around the house in black socks, undershorts, and fedora, like Michel Piccoli. *Contempt*, too, ends with two lovers in a fatal car wreck, although Bardot there plays a passive, done-unto character.

    The prevalent interpretation that has Maria representing a soulless, rapacious Germany on the make is at odds both with the character's virtues and with Schygulla's radiant performance. In period dress, taking her cocky, wide-legged stance, she looks like a cross between Grable and Stanwyck. If she's a Teutonic Scarlett O'Hara, grubbing her way back after a war, it's Scarlett

O'Hara without lies and conniving betrayals. Fassbinder usually used Schygulla like this, as a glowing life force and an incorruptible outsider.

Lili Marleen, too, begins with a thwarted marriage. This time, the lovers in bed (Schygulla's Willie and Giancarlo Giannini's Robert) are interrupted by an emissary from Robert's father—it's tempting to write, from The Father. Mel Ferrer's erect, silver-haired patriarch, a Swiss-German Jew, sits at the top of finance, culture, politics, religion, and morality. Little Robert doesn't stand a chance when his father wants the German, non-Jewish Willie out of the picture. (Fassbinder's mother plays Robert's silent mother, in thrall to her husband.) Indeed, Giannini is photographed mostly in terms of his woeful-puppy eyes; in the end, a famous orchestra conductor and reconciled with his father, he's become a self-absorbed buffoon. The irony both this film and Maria Braun underline is that the love object is inadequate; the woman saves herself for nothing.

Willie is Robert's temperamental opposite: irrepressible, buoyant, fearless, inner-directed, and, like Maria Braun, totally faithful to "her man," even if she does sell her body. Both movies end with a pact between the Fathers (the meeting between the Swiss Jews and the Nazis over the gorge is symbolic), one that dooms the free-spirited and unobedient. The difference between these two and earlier films is that although the hero is doomed, she is Promethian.

Lili Marleen is built around a ballad. Like Herr R.'s vaguely remembered tune (standing for the mother's lullaby), it's "a very sad song sung with lots of feeling." Although "Lili Marleen," also called "The Sentry's Song," has to do with the wartime separation of lovers, Fassbinder's song emphasizes the bond between parents and children, and particularly mothers and sons. (When the lovers in the movie kiss and part, a nearby mother and son do the same.) Soldiers at the front, from all nations, leave off fighting when they hear it. "My God, I sing a song—a song, that's all," says Willie when Robert confronts her for working with Nazis. "You enjoy it," he accuses her. "I do," she replies. The song is banned for decadence and morbidity when it's clear that the sentiment behind it—pure longing—breaks down Nazi order and belligerence. At one of Willie's performances, a Nazi officer finds himself wearing a feather boa.

Wo ist Lili, today? Scorned by critics, Lili Marleen isn't even available on videotape in the United States. Like its protagonist, it seems to have faded into oblivion. Curiously, the last time I saw the film was five years ago in Prague, a city, like postwar Berlin, recovering from its own trauma. Perhaps the work means more to people who have suffered under a great oppression. Here, Fassbinder bound is valued more than Fassbinder free.

1. In a 1971 interview with Christian Braad Thomsen, Fassbinder remarked that "a European director is not as naive as a Hollywood director . . . though I am sure the day will come when I, too, shall be able to tell a perfectly naive story." Elsewhere, Fassbinder is quoted as saying, "I would not be able to tell a film like Marnie simply, the way Hitchcock does it, because I haven't got the courage of his naivety . . . maybe one day I'll have that courage myself" (Thomas Elsaesser, "A Cinema of Vicious Circles," in Tony Rayns, ed., Fassbinder [London: British Film Institute, 1976], p. 31).

Margit Carstensen,
RWF on the set of
*Bremer Freiheit
(Bremen Freedom)*, 1972

*Die Sehnsucht der
Veronika Voss (Veronika
Voss)*. 1982. Rosel Zech

The Forward-looking Traditionalist
Wolfram Schütte

In the mid-1960s, when Bertolt Brecht's Epic Theater dominated the German-speaking stage, Max Frisch spoke of Brecht possessing the "striking ineffectiveness of a classic." The playwright, who agitated for social change in epic parables written for a "theater of the scientific age," was accepted by society and integrated into it, and was thus a classic: immobilized. Rainer Werner Fassbinder, who attained comparable artistic status in the German-language cinema between 1969 and 1982, and whose public image dominated the scene during those fourteen years, neither became a classic nor did he achieve outstanding success. But was he ineffective?

Looking down at the lamentable depth of contemporary German cinema from the aesthetic summit of his late works, after the 1978 *Despair*, and from the paradigmatic validity of his "German" subjects, from *Katzelmacher* to *Veronika Voss*, one will scarcely discern anything in the ten years since he died except his disappearance: not only the dissolution of Fassbinder as a steady presence, somewhat like the basso continuo in the polyphony of the German cinema that came after him, but the general decline of all aesthetic principles that blossomed in the richness of his vast oeuvre.

Fassbinder's oeuvre, like that of other directors of the New German Cinema, could not have come about without the cooperation of the public television stations. Yet he, as did no other, realized the implications of the specifically German production situation. His artistic productivity, which resulted in an oeuvre of forty-four film and television productions, coincided with the vigorous appropriation and exploitation of every possible source he could draw from. He alone gave exuberant life to the declaration on which the Young and the New German Cinema staked its claim, that "*Opas Kino*" (grandpa's cinema) was dead. If there was a German Autorenfilm (auteurist cinema)—and certainly the genius-cult of West German Sturm und Drang in the 1960s and 1970s did produce the works of Kluge and Wenders, Schroeter and von Praunheim, Herzog and Syberberg, Thome and Straub—Fassbinder's far-reaching activities were at the center of it.

His genius—probably the only one of the postwar German cinema—is evident not only in his work but also in the freewheeling activity and inspirational vitality with which he combined film and film production, television and television production into a comprehensive, always expanding, retrospective, and progressive unity. His utopian vision, which he very nearly made come true, was to merge the division of labor of the studio system with the author's personal creativity through an amalgamation of group dynamics and individualistic work processes. He was producer-tycoon and star director all in one; and to feed the artistic imagination that spurred him on, he needed to make sure that he kept both feet on the ground. This he first achieved with the team of the Action Theater, in the group which evolved from it, and later in various teams of actors, cinematographers, musicians, set designers, and studios.

The auteurist film, whose emergence accompanied the decline of the "producer-film" that could no longer compete with television in the domestic market, was unmistakably a harbinger of the antiauthoritarian movement and an expression of the international student and youth revolt, which in the Paris of May 1968 had its storming of the Bastille and, shortly after, its Thermidor and Waterloo. Euphoria over a new lifestyle was rapidly succeeded by depression over its failure—more quickly, in keeping with the modern process of acceleration, than at the turn of the eighteenth to the nineteenth century. The socialist-liberal coalition; the ban on employment of radicals in state schools and public institutions in general; the German Director's Theater of Peter Stein, Claus Peymann, and Hans Neuenfels; and the New German Cinema were parallel events, riddled by the ricochets of Baader-Meinhof terrorism.

Rainer Werner Fassbinder, born in 1945, was not one of the initiators of the Oberhausen Manifesto. He did not subscribe to their programmatic approach, in which German postwar film history was understood largely as a continuation of UFA films (Universum-Film AG, or UFA, was the principal film company in Germany before 1945) and as a product of the Adenauer-era restoration. Nor did he adopt Alexander Kluge's idea of a conscious return to authentic, documentary-oriented contemporary film subjects. Fassbinder, as the youngest, had only recently become one of the West German filmmakers, and he was and always remained an outsider. His roots were in the theater rather than in documentary, industrial, art, or television filmmaking. In the theater, as director, actor, and author, as spiritus rector, he gathered around him a troupe.

In the course of his filmmaking career, Fassbinder's involvement with the theater ended—definitely by 1974–75, when he foundered with the management of the TAT (Theater am Turm) in Frankfurt, which he had tried to develop into a base for parallel film production. He nevertheless succeeded where comparable movie talents, like Peter Stein and Luc Bondy, had failed, in finding the royal road to developing his artistic potential in film. The theater of Stein, Bondy, and Hans Neuenfels repeatedly cast envious glances toward the cinema, whose character as a total work of art these directors evoked on stage; yet only with Fassbinder did the theater open its eyes wide, because in his films it plays a vital role (as it does in those of Visconti).

With one other German-speaking artist, namely Peter Handke, whose often-professed love of the cinema he has frequently brought to the work of his spiritually congenial friend Wim Wenders, Fassbinder shared a talent that the stage directors Stein, Neuenfels, and Bondy did not have at their disposal: an innate narrative creativity. It is this that accounts for Fassbinder's unique status, the concentrated density of his filmic oeuvre, and it is this—despite craftsmanly equivalents, for example in the work of Volker Schlöndorff or Reinhard Hauff—that fundamentally sets him apart. He is also set apart from the storytellers of the New German Cinema insofar as this teller of his own tale was able to handle his own material and subject matter in an aesthetically far-more-intimate and personal way, or, to paraphrase Kleist, he was able to recognize the cinematographic potential of his stories, "formulating his ideas while he

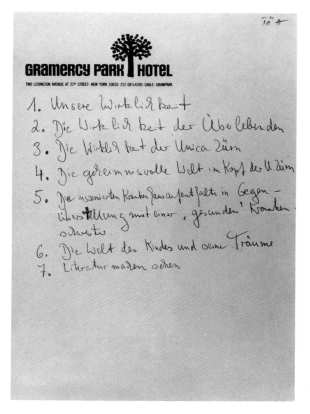

Notes by RWF for an unrealized film about the Swiss writer Unica Zürn, who committed suicide in 1970. 1978

was talking"; in short, he did not think of storytelling in film as adapting literature to the medium of vision and sound but was able to think in cinematographic terms from the start.

This genuine filmic creativity comprehends the "straightaway" of Raoul Walsh and Michael Curtiz in the same sovereign manner as the lighting direction of Josef von Sternberg, the color dramaturgy of Douglas Sirk, and Joseph L. Mankiewicz's complex narrative strategies (as a creative counterpart, for instance, of the Döblinesque montage technique in *Berlin Alexanderplatz*). This, in particular, made possible Fassbinder adaptations of literary sources (as with *Effi Briest*, *The Stationmaster's Wife*, *Querelle*), where—each in its own way—no residue of the adaptation process remains to disturb or irritate.

Nevertheless, the theater from which he grew and eventually escaped shaped the director's style, determined the stringency of his storytelling and the visual concentration of his work. The stage as the scene of action, as the conceptual abstraction of a lived life, returns even in apparently naturalistic movies, such as *The Merchant of Four Seasons*, *Ali: Fear Eats the Soul*, *Fear of Fear*, or *I Only Want You to Love Me*, through a nonnaturalistic mode of speech. He signals distance, irritation with realistic events, which are—to a greater extent than stage scenery would permit—charged with additional narrative value through a metaphoric use of camera angles. This is why one finds more than one sees and hears in Fassbinder's "realistic works"; and this is what distinguishes his films from the numerous "realistic" movies about the workers' world, by which a part of the New German Cinema turned its attention, polemically and functionally, to the everyday lives of the working-class petit bourgeoisie.

What Fassbinder learned from and taught was theater as the preschool of film dialogue, which must lose its clarity in visual montage and gain incidental redundancy; what Fassbinder

discovered for the New German Cinema, and developed inimitably and with a virtuosity like no other, was theater as the presence of actor-characters, as physicality in space. Part of his indisputable genius can be seen in those countless moments when he enticed actors into playing roles in which they would attain the human dignity of unforgettable characters, whether in a minor part or as stars. It did not matter whether the actors were unknown or already well established—whether their names were Kurt Raab, Hanna Schygulla, Gottfried John, or Günter Lamprecht. This Pygmalion made them all come alive—admittedly sometimes only for those brief moments when his eyes lit on them and inspired them to epiphanies of his personal obsessions, obsessions with characters. They were not "made" by the camera, lighting, color, scenery, and editing. These elements just created the "aura" in which, thanks to their personal presence, they appeared on film.

Paradoxically enough, the rupture that isolated Fassbinder's oeuvre within the New German (i.e., West German) Cinema was caused by his own ardent traditionalism. Yet it was from this traditionalism that his aesthetic richness flowed. While his Oberhausen Group comrades and older contemporaries wanted, with their *Abschied von Gestern* (the German title of Alexander Kluge's *Yesterday Girl*; literally, "goodbye to yesterday"), to make a radical break with the past, with UFA and its renewal and extension in the postwar era, with German regional kitsch and "problem" movies, Fassbinder would not settle for that. The members of the Oberhausen Group did not believe that there was a German tradition they could relate to, since this tradition had compromised itself through aesthetic and political collaboration with fascism, nor did any of them in those days dream of imitating Hollywood. To be sure, Wenders would later confess his reverence for Lang, Ozu, Ford, and Nicholas Ray; Herzog for Murnau and the German Expressionist cinema; Kluge for Vertov, Eisenstein, and Godard; Thome for Hawks; and Straub for Bresson and Dreyer. Yet in the "fatherless society," as psychoanalyst Alexander Mitscherlich called it in his analysis of contemporary West Germany, the artists acted as though they were starting from square one. Was this a late counterpart to the movement in postwar literature, which sought to make a fresh start after the "zero hour" of 1945?

In the midst of German self-alienation as a fatherless people who had also lost their fatherland, Fassbinder offered a scandalous, wishful father relationship, hardly taken seriously or even understood by his contemporaries. His favorite saint was a Dane who, under the name of Detlef Sierck, had made *Schlussakkord* (1936), *Zu neuen Ufern* (1937), and *La Habanera* (1937) for UFA and as Douglas Sirk had filmed in Hollywood *Imitation of Life* (1959), *All That Heaven Allows* (1955), and *Written on the Wind* (1956), among others—movies, discovered by the young film buffs in puberty, to whose impassioned palette of suffering, oppression, and despair Fassbinder remained true, tried to emulate exactly this cinema about people and their confused feelings. His fascination with Sirk was a fascination also with melodrama. Of the infamous seductions of the Hollywood dream factory, it is one of the most notorious genres of false sentiment, clichés of the soul, and fuzzy perception. At least that was how the Oberhausen group saw it, as did many of the film critics who shared their view.

Fassbinder made his debut with melodramas frozen to a cynical iciness, incongruously realized as gangster movies, "bande-à-part" pictures, set in the suburbs of Munich (*Love Is Colder Than Death*; *Gods of the Plague*; *Rio das Mortes*; *The American Soldier*). But with *Why Does Herr R. Run Amok?* in 1970 and the pseudo-Western *Whity* in 1971, he emerged as a chamber-drama melodramatist, and with *Recruits in Ingolstadt* and *The Merchant of Four Seasons* he turned to social melodrama that would remain unique. The characters who appeared in those movies did not immediately become specimens to be examined under the crosshairs of social analysis. Precisely because Fassbinder set his melodramas in the petit bourgeois milieu of the working class (right up to *Berlin Alexanderplatz*)—and thereby opened new social territory for the West German cinema, which it would lose again after his death—he left the orbit of autobiography, subjective obsessions, from which the *Autorenfilm* had emerged, and into which it subsequently decayed, sinking ever more deeply into an artistic Bohemia of petty relationships, and thus into the teary self-reflections of the filmmaker.

"All I know about is people," Fassbinder once said, but he knew them well, and he fathomed them as did no one else. The "generator of feelings" that Kluge saw at work in the opera, and whose dangerous, catastrophic threat he sought to "defuse" by enlightening the audience, was regarded by Fassbinder (whose favorite opera was *La Traviata*), as a relay station for the human capacity to suffer and endure; as the battlefield of a war taking place daily and hourly between people and within them, in living rooms and apartments, in glances exchanged, boxed into small squares, refracted and reflected in mirrors, steeped in color and light and illuminated by them. The dialectic of "false" and "true" feelings, their shifting and warping over time, the complexity and complicity of lovers and loved ones, speaks: victims and perpetrators, the exposure of the stigmata of the soul and its wounds, the permanence of violence in love relationships—that was his narrative domain, which he could extract as easily from a newspaper item as from Fontane's *Effi Briest* or Genet's *Querelle*.

He was aiming for a "comédie humaine"—preferably under German conditions—both historical and up-to-the-minute. When he spoke of Hollywood, he thought of material and subjects that were personally developed and collectively put across, because they dealt with collective traumas, popular myths of everyday life, the "false life" (Adorno) and those things experienced and articulated as kitsch that went with it. Admittedly, this did not take the form of naturalistic imitation, but neither was it the gesture of a Godardian quotation. The reconstruction of moments in history—whether set in the nineteenth century as in *Effi Briest*, the Nazi–UFA period as in *Lili Marleen*, the postwar era as in *The Marriage of Maria Braun*, or the

German economic boom as in *Lola*—simultaneously reflected contemporary visual and acoustic codes and standards in photography, cinema, radio, and fashion.

Historical recollections seen through the veil of mass media's development, cinema as a screen on which to project the modes of experience typical of a particular age: this more than any aesthetic program can be recognized as the essential underlying theme in Fassbinder's oeuvre. In addition to this renewal of tradition, this re-inventorying of a medium, he found a place in his work to realize the potential of acting in post–UFA-period German films—not stigmatizing acting by diminishing it, as the New German Cinema generally did, but integrating into his own work actors and actresses who were better than the movies they had previously or recently appeared in. In this way he again reconnected with a broken line of tradition.

Throughout Fassbinder's work one can almost speak of a reconciliation between the young and the old, to which the appearances and leading performances of Luise Ulrich or Werner Finck, Brigitte Mira and Karlheinz Böhm, Barbara Valentin and Adrian Hoven, among others, greatly contributed. This ideologically unprejudiced attitude reflected not only his keen personal interest in professional actors but also his need for older actors who could cut across generational lines. Because the movies also addressed an older generation, they gained an audience that extended beyond the small circle of the New German Cinema, whose fans were mostly youthful.

Fassbinder's intense need "to do something in order to feel alive" could not have been fulfilled had he not been endowed with the strategic ability to coordinate his Balzacian creative energy with the division of labor which is part of the process of film and television production. In other words, the continuity of his narrative film oeuvre basically required the framework of a movie industry, which had ceased to exist with the collapse of West German film production. The *Autorenfilm* was not only the genius-cult postulate of a generation which no longer wanted anything to do with the West German way of movie making (preferring to go to the street rather than stay in the studios), but also the product of an artificially induced movie shortage.

Television, as a substitute producer that has no need to take account of the film producer's business calculations, released the New German Cinema from the dictates of the market; working in cooperation with it, the West German Film Promotion Board established a culturally defined (i.e., not market-oriented) safety zone where the phenomenon of the internationally recognized and much admired New German Cinema could flourish. On the one hand, this model of promoting movie production was responsible for the dazzling diversity of German film talent, yet it eventually caused an artificial boom. In the course of a surreptitious but increasingly obvious competition in commercialization between public and private television companies and a regionalization of film promotion (owing to its federal character, West Germany did not have a centralized cultural authority), the sponsorship system, which still functioned in Fassbinder's time, became largely counterproductive. A maze of red tape led to collective and individual delays in production, making continuity of work practically impossible.

This also led to a dissipation of what might be called the infrastructural surplus value that Fassbinder's steady mode of production had generated for the German cinema—that is, a professionalization in all areas of film and television production. Through his team-based method of production, he not only discovered actors for the German cinema and brought them close to stardom—for example, Hanna Schygulla and Barbara Sukowa, Günter Lamprecht and Klaus Löwitsch—he also helped to develop the talents of cinematographers like Michael Ballhaus and Xaver Schwarzenberger, editors like Juliane Lorenz, costume designers like Barbara Baum, and musicians like Peer Raben.

One sees the aim, in all the activities of Fassbinder—who, faced with the decision whether to shoot on location or in the studio, decided not on ideological but practical grounds—

of singlehandedly developing a film-industry method of production from which everyone would benefit through the increased professionalization it would bring about. But since the New German Cinema, its authors, producers, and critics, were neither willing nor possibly even able to recognize Fassbinder's all-out programmatic traditionalism as a possible model for national film production, his singlehanded effort ultimately remained without significant consequences.

Only this friction—the nature of public cinema—would have allowed vigor, robustness, and accessibility to develop through experience, just as national and individual talents can develop only in a competitive environment. In contrast to Alexander Kluge's programmatic solution—when in danger and distress, it is death to take the middle way—Fassbinder's lonely search for means of production was directed at the center of a possible future. In his case, the "middle way" was the "impure cinema," which continuously meanders through the gamut of possibilities offered by genres as well as the modes of production and reception, and in the course of its "zigzagging through the institutions" becomes professionalized, ingenious, crafty, knowledgable, and imaginative—only this "impure," even unscrupulous Fassbinder cinema could be the way of the future; and his hard-earned solidity allowed true solidarity only with those whose singular artistic sensibility needed everyone's protection.

For Fassbinder's genius was not just his art, but—to an equal degree—the path he took. This path is still open to those who may not have his genius, but who can become artists all the same. They will have to stand and be tested, as he did, come hell or high water. This is not just a question of courage and boldness, but of dignity. Anyone who can imagine himself only as failing in the process lacks the imagination to fall in love with success: even at the price of failure.

Filmography 1966–82

This Night	1966
Der Stadtstreicher	*The City Tramp* 1966
Das kleine Chaos	*The Little Chaos* 1967
Liebe ist kälter als der Tod	*Love Is Colder Than Death* 1969
Katzelmacher	1969
Götter der Pest	*Gods of the Plague* 1969
Warum läuft Herr R. Amok?	*Why Does Herr R. Run Amok?* 1969
Rio das Mortes	1970
Das Kaffeehaus	*The Coffeehouse* 1970
Whity	1970
Die Niklashauser Fart	*The Niklashausen Journey* 1970
Warnung vor einer heiligen Nutte	*Beware of a Holy Whore* 1970
Der Amerikanische Soldat	*The American Soldier* 1970
Pioniere in Ingolstadt	*Recruits in Ingolstadt* 1970
Händler der vier Jahreszeiten	*The Merchant of Four Seasons* 1971
Die bitteren Tränen der Petra von Kant	*The Bitter Tears of Petra von Kant* 1972
Wildwechsel	*Jail Bait* 1972
Acht Stunden sind kein Tag	*Eight Hours Don't Make a Day* 1972
Bremer Freiheit	*Bremen Freedom* 1972
Welt am Draht	*World on a Wire* 1973
Nora Helmer	1973
Angst essen Seele auf	*Ali: Fear Eats the Soul* 1973
Martha	1973
Fontane Effi Briest	*Effi Briest* 1972/74
Faustrecht der Freiheit	*Fox and His Friends* 1974
Wie ein Vogel auf dem Draht	*Like a Bird on a Wire* 1974
Mutter Küsters' Fahrt zum Himmel	*Mother Küsters Goes to Heaven* 1975
Angst vor der Angst	*Fear of Fear* 1975
Ich will doch nur, dass Ihr mich liebt	*I Only Want You to Love Me* 1975
Satansbraten	*Satan's Brew* 1976
Chinesisches Roulette	*Chinese Roulette* 1976
Bolwieser	*The Stationmaster's Wife* 1977/83
Frauen in New York	*Women in New York* 1977
Despair—Eine Reise ins Licht	*Despair* 1977
Episode of **Deutschland im Herbst**	*Germany in Autumn* 1978
Die Ehe der Maria Braun	*The Marriage of Maria Braun* 1978
In einem Jahr mit 13 Monden	*In a Year of 13 Moons* 1978
Die dritte Generation	*The Third Generation* 1978/79
Berlin Alexanderplatz	1979/80
Lili Marleen	1980
Lola	1981
Theater in Trance	1981
Die Sehnsucht der Veronika Voss	*Veronika Voss* 1982

1966
This Night
No copy of this short film, made in July 1966, is known to exist.

SCREENPLAY AND CAMERA: Rainer Werner Fassbinder. Color, 8mm.

1966
Der Stadtstreicher
(The City Tramp)
A tramp finds a pistol in an alley and tries to get rid of it.

Roser-Film.
SCREENPLAY: Rainer Werner Fassbinder. **CAMERA:** Josef Jung.

With Christoph Roser (the tramp), Susanne Schimkus (maid), Michael Fengler, Thomas Fengler, Irm Hermann, Rainer Werner Fassbinder (young man in a leather jacket).
Shot in Munich, November 1966. B/W, 16mm.
10 minutes.

1967
Das kleine Chaos
(The Little Chaos)
Three young people pretending to sell magazine subscriptions attempt a swindle.

Roser-Film.
SCREENPLAY: Rainer Werner Fassbinder. **CAMERA:** Michael Fengler. **SOUND:** Armin Athanassious.

With Rainer Werner Fassbinder (Franz), Marite Greiselis (Marite), Christoph Roser (Theo), Greta Rehfeld, Lilo Pempeit.
Shot in Munich, February 1967. B/W, 35mm.
9 minutes.

1969
Liebe ist kälter als der Tod
(Love Is Colder than Death)
Franz, a small-time pimp attached to the whore Joanna, resists joining the syndicate. Franz loves another criminal, the handsome murderer Bruno, and they plan to rob a bank together. The film is dedicated to "Claude Chabrol, Eric Rohmer, Jean-Marie Straub, Linio and Cuncho." The last two names are characters in the 1966 Italian film by Damiano Damiani, *Quios Sabe?*

Antiteater-X-Film.
SCREENPLAY: Rainer Werner Fassbinder. **CAMERA:** Dietrich Lohmann. **ASS'T CAMERA:** Herbert Paetzold. **EDITING:** *Franz Walsch* (i.e., Rainer Werner Fassbinder). **LIGHTING:** Peter Wagner. **ART DIRECTION:** Ulli Lommel and Rainer Werner Fassbinder. **SOUND:** Gottfried Hüngsberg. **MUSIC:** Peer Raben and Holger Münzer. **ASS'T DIRECTOR:** Martin Müller. **PROD'N MANAGERS:** Christian Hohoff and *Wil Rabenbauer* (i.e., Peer Raben).

With Ulli Lommel (Bruno), Hanna Schygulla (Joanna), Rainer Werner Fassbinder (Franz), Hans Hirschmüller (Peter), Peter Berling (Schuster), Ingrid Caven (second prostitute), Irm Hermann (saleslady), Kurt Raab (warehouse detective), Yaak Karsunke (police commissioner).
Shot in Munich, April 1969. B/W, 35mm. 88 minutes.

1969
Katzelmacher
Jorgos is a young Greek guest worker in Germany, known pejoratively as a "Katzelmacher," Bavarian slang for "cat screwer," referring to the supposed sexual habits of foreigners. He rents a room in Elisabeth's house in the Munich suburbs. She and Peter hang around with a group of disaffected and bored young people who resent Jorgos and beat him up when he goes out with a German girl.

Antiteater-X-Film.
SCREENPLAY: Rainer Werner Fassbinder. **CAMERA:** Dietrich Lohmann. **ASS'T CAMERA:** Herbert Paetzold. **EDITING:** *Franz Walsch* (i.e., Rainer Werner Fassbinder). **ART DIRECTION:** Rainer Werner Fassbinder. **SOUND:** Gottfried Hüngsberg. **MUSIC:** Peer Raben. **ASS'T DIRECTOR:** Michael Fengler. **PROD'N MANAGERS:** *Wil Rabenbauer* (i.e., Peer Raben) and Christian Hohoff.

With Hanna Schygulla (Marie), Lilith Ungerer (Helga), Elga Sorbas (Rosy), Doris Mattes (Gunda), Rainer Werner Fassbinder (Jorgos), Harry Baer (Franz), Peter Moland (Peter), Irm Hermann (Elisabeth), Rudolf Waldemar Brem (Paul), Hans Hirschmüller (Eric), Hannes Gromball (Klaus)

Christoph Roser

"The first films I directed more to gain some practical knowledge and a way of approaching film. At that time film for me was also more concrete than literature. I probably would have been scarcely able to adapt a film from literature, since the theme of my films was primarily the experience of movies, by me and by the viewer."

RWF, 1971

RWF

"In my films there shouldn't be feelings that people already have digested or absorbed; the film should create new ones instead."

RWF, 1969

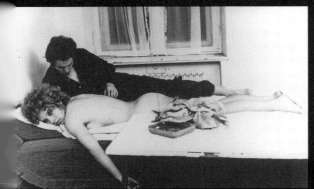

Hanna Schygulla, Ulli Lommel

"Much in the first nine [full-length] films up to *Beware of a Holy Whore* satisfied me quite simply because the films expressed my situation at that time very concretely. . . . If you see them together, it becomes clear that they were made by someone who put into them his sensibility, his aggressiveness, and his fear. Nonetheless, I don't quite count these first nine movies; they are too elitist and too private, and they actually were made only for us and for

1969

Götter der Pest
(Gods of the Plague)

Taciturn Franz Walsch, fresh out of prison, visits Joanna, his girlfriend. He is implicated in his brother's murder and has affairs with other women. He resumes his relationship with his buddy the hoodlum Günther, known as "Gorilla," and together they plan a supermarket robbery. They are betrayed, and the police lie in wait.

Antiteater-X-Film.
SCREENPLAY: Rainer Werner Fassbinder. **CAMERA:** Dietrich Lohmann. **ASS'T CAMERA:** Herbert Paetzold. **EDITING:** *Franz Walsch* (i.e., Rainer Werner Fassbinder) and Thea Eymèsz. **LIGHTING:** Ekkehard Heinrich. **ART DIRECTION:** Kurt Raab. **SOUND:** Gottfried Hüngsberg. **MUSIC:** Peer Raben. **ASS'T DIRECTOR:** Kurt Raab. **PROD'N MANAGERS:** Peer Raben and Christian Hohoff.

With Harry Baer (Franz), Hanna Schygulla (Joanna), Margarethe von Trotta (Margarethe), Günther Kaufmann (Günther), Ingrid Caven (Magdalena Fuller), Carla Aulaulu (Carla), Lilo Pempeit (mother), Rainer Werner Fassbinder (porno salesman).
Shot in Munich, October–November 1969. B/W, 35mm. 91 minutes.

1969

Warum läuft Herr R. Amok?
(Why Does Herr R. Run Amok?)

Herr R., a mild man, is a draftsman for an architectural firm. He does his work every day and returns home to his wife and young son every evening. They talk about his imminent promotion, money, television, and food. One night a neighbor comes to chat with Frau R. while her husband tries to watch television. Annoyed, Herr R. suddenly brings down the chandelier.

Antiteater/Maran-Film, in association with Süddeutscher Rundfunk.
CO-DIRECTOR: Michael Fengler. **SCREENPLAY:** improvised by Michael Fengler and Rainer Werner Fassbinder. **CAMERA:** Dietrich Lohmann. **ASS'T CAMERA:** Herbert Paetzold. **EDITING:** *Franz Walsch* (i.e., Rainer Werner Fassbinder) and Michael Fengler. **LIGHTING:** Ekkehard Heinrich. **ART DIRECTION:** Kurt Raab. **SOUND:** Klaus Eckelt, assisted by Franz Pusl. **MUSIC:** Peer Raben. **ASS'T DIRECTOR:** Harry Baer. **PROD'N MANAGERS:** *Wilhelm Rabenbauer* (Peer Raben) and Christian Hohoff.

With Kurt Raab (Herr R.), Lilith Ungerer (his wife), Amadeus Fengler (their son), Franz Maron (chef), Hanna Schygulla (school friend), Harry Baer/Peter Moland/Lilo Pempeit (colleagues at the office), Ingrid Caven, Doris Mattes, Irm Hermann, and Hannes Gromball (neighbors).
Shot in Munich, December 1969. Color, 35mm (filmed in 16mm). 88 minutes.

1970

Rio das Mortes

Two young friends, Michel, a tile layer, and Günther, fresh from military duty, decide to leave Germany in search of a treasure they believe to be hidden in the Rio das Mortes area of Peru. Hanna, Michel's fiancée, opposes this plan and threatens to shoot them both if they embark on this childish adventure.

Janus Film und Fernsehen/Antiteater-X-Film.
SCREENPLAY: Rainer Werner Fassbinder, from an idea by Volker Schlöndorff. **CAMERA:** Dietrich Lohmann. **ASS'T CAMERA:** Herbert Paetzold. **EDITING:** Thea Eymèsz. **LIGHTING:** Ekkehard Heinrich. **ART DIRECTION:** Kurt Raab. **MUSIC:** Peer Raben. **ASS'T DIRECTORS:** Kurt Raab and Harry Baer. **PROD'N MANAGER:** Michael Fengler.

With Hanna Schygulla (Hanna), Michael König (Michel), Günther Kaufmann (Günther), Katrin Schaake (Katrin), Joachim von Mengershausen (Joachim), Lilo Pempeit (Günther's mother), Harry Baer (Michel's colleague), Carla Aulaulu (Maggie), Ulli Lommel (auto salesman), Rainer Werner Fassbinder (disco customer), Ingrid Caven, Magdalena Montezuma.
Shot in Munich, January 1970. Color, 16mm. 84 minutes.

Harry Baer, Ingrid Caven

"*Gods of the Plague* is a rather precise film about the feeling of a certain period of time, the way things really were in that peculiar postrevolutionary era of 1970."

RWF, 1978

Kurt Raab

"In *Katzelmacher* we wanted to offer an alternative viewpoint through the style, and in *Amok* through the use of color as well; the audience should understand the content and see that it relates to them, while at the same time, through the form by which it is communicated, they gain some distance so that they can reflect on what they're seeing."

RWF, 1970

"The film works with movie experience, with things that seem great in movies, things you've learned in movies; from another angle, though, it tells a story that has quite a lot to do with reality: the people are in the midst of a specific work process and are, as characters, presented rather differently than is the case elsewhere in my films, I mean in the theatrical movies, where how they live and what they do for a living is not as important as how they feel."

RWF, 1971

Michael König

1970
Das Kaffeehaus
(The Coffeehouse)

In Ridolfo's coffeehouse, citizens meet to talk about money, friendship, love, and honor. This is a modernistic staging for television of a play by Carlo Goldoni (1707–1793), the Venetian playwright whose many works preserve in scripted form the improvisational productions of the Italian commedia dell'arte.

Westdeutscher Rundfunk. Produced by antiteater, Munich, in association with the Bremen Schauspielhaus, Concordia.
TELEPLAY: Rainer Werner Fassbinder, from Carlo Goldoni. CAMERA: Dietbert Schmidt and Manfred Förster. ART DIRECTION: Wilfried Minks. MUSIC: Peer Raben.

With Margit Carstensen (Vittoria), Ingrid Caven (Placida), Hanna Schygulla (Lisaura), Kurt Raab (Don Marzio), Harry Baer (Eugenio), Hans Hirschmüller (Trappolo), Günther Kaufmann (Leander).
Shot in Cologne, February 1970. B/W, video. 105 minutes.

1970
Whity

Somewhere in the American West in 1878, in a large house that is more like a mausoleum than a home, lives the Nicholson family. It includes Ben, the domineering patriarch; Katherine, his second wife, a nymphomaniac; and his two sons by his first wife, Frank, a homosexual, and Davy, who is mentally retarded. Serving and being abused by the family is a young black man, Whity, Ben's illegitimate son who wants to belong.

Atlantis Film/Antiteater-X-Film.
SCREENPLAY: Rainer Werner Fassbinder. CAMERA: Michael Ballhaus. ASS'T CAMERA: Lothar Dreher. EDITING: Franz Walsch (i.e., Rainer Werner Fassbinder) and Thea Eymèsz. LIGHTING: Honorat Stangl. ART DIRECTION: Kurt Raab. MUSIC: Peer Raben. ASS'T DIRECTOR: Harry Baer. PROD'N MANAGERS: Peter Berling, Stefan Abendroth, and Martin Köberle.

With Günther Kaufmann (Whity), Hanna Schygulla (Hanna), Ulli Lommel (Frank), Harry Baer (Davy), Katrin Schaake (Katherine), Ron Randell (Ben Nicholson), Kurt Raab (pianist), Rainer Werner Fassbinder (man in saloon).
Shot in Almería, Spain, April 1970. Color, 35mm, CinemaScope. 95 minutes.

1970
Die Niklashauser Fart
(The Niklashausen Journey)

On March 3, 1476, a shepherd, Hans Böhm, claimed in Niklashausen to have seen the Mother of God. He gathered around him thirty thousand peasants who believed Böhm to be the New Messiah. He preached a doctrine against vested privilege that was revolutionary. He was arrested by the bishop and burned at the stake in Würzburg on July 15, five months after his vision. The film is not a historical reënactment but Fassbinder's essay on the application of the past to the present.

Janus Film und Fernsehen, in association with Westdeutscher Rundfunk.
CO-DIRECTOR: Michael Fengler. SCREENPLAY: Rainer Werner Fassbinder and Michael Fengler. CAMERA: Dietrich Lohmann. EDITING: Franz Walsch (i.e., Rainer Werner Fassbinder) and Thea Eymèsz. LIGHTING: Honorat Stangl. SPECIAL EFFECTS: Charly Baumgartner. ART DIRECTION: Kurt Raab. MUSIC: Peer Raben and Amon Düül II. ASS'T DIRECTOR: Harry Baer.

With Michael König (Hans Böhm), Michael Gordon (Antonio), Rainer Werner Fassbinder (black monk), Hanna Schygulla (Johanna), Margit Carstensen (Margarethe), Kurt Raab (bishop), Günther Kaufmann (peasant leader), Ingrid Caven (screaming girl), Carla Aulaulu (epileptic), Peer Raben (monsignor).
Shot in Munich, Starnberg, and Feldkirchen, May 1970. Color, 16mm. 86 minutes.

Ingrid Caven, Margit Carstensen, Rudolf Waldemar Brem, Peer Raben,
Harry Baer, Hans Hirschmüller

"Yet in actual fact, the entire film is pitted against the black man, because he always hesitates and fails to defend himself against injustice. In the end he does shoot the people who oppressed him, but then he goes off into the desert and dies, having come to realize certain things without being able to act. He goes into the desert because he doesn't dare face the inevitable consequences. I find it OK that he kills his oppressors, but it is not OK that he then goes into the desert. For by doing that he accepts the superiority of the others. Had he truly believed in his action, he would have allied himself with other suppressed individuals, and they would have acted together. The single-handed act at the end of the movie is not a solution. Thus, in the last instance the film turns even against blacks."

RWF, 1971

Günther Kaufmann, Hanna Schygulla

Michael König, Hanna Schygulla

"We didn't want to make a historical film but instead wanted to show how and why a revolution fails. For that we had to consciously demolish every historical limitation that would restrict us. The viewer shouldn't get the notion, Oh yeah, that happened in 1476. An idea like that would tranquilize him, and instead he should be disturbed as he watches."

RWF, 1970

1970
Warnung vor einer heiligen Nutte
(Beware of a Holy Whore)

A film's crew and cast, including Eddie Constantine, sit around a seedy seaside hotel in Spain waiting for the film's director to start shooting. Meanwhile, the production manager bullies everyone and sexual intrigues develop at the hotel bar. These are compounded when the director finally arrives.

Antiteater-X-Film/Nova International. SCREENPLAY: Rainer Werner Fassbinder. CAMERA: Michael Ballhaus. EDITING: *Franz Walsch* (i.e., Rainer Werner Fassbinder) and Thea Eymèsz. ART DIRECTION: Kurt Raab. MUSIC: Peer Raben. ASS'T DIRECTOR: Harry Baer. PROD'N MANAGERS: Michael Fengler and Christian Hohoff.

With Lou Castel (Jeff), Eddie Constantine (as himself), Hanna Schygulla (Hanna), Marquard Bohm (Ricky), Rainer Werner Fassbinder (Sascha), Ulli Lommel (Korbinian), Margarethe von Trotta (production secretary).
Shot in Sorrento, Italy, September 1970. Color, 35mm. 103 minutes.

1970
Der Amerikanische Soldat
(The American Soldier)

Ricky, a small-time American gangster who has served in Vietnam, returns to Munich where he grew up and where he is wanted by the police. Working as a hired killer, Ricky fulfills some assignments, spends some time in childhood haunts with his friend Franz Walsch, visits his mother and brother, waits in his hotel room, murders his whorish mistress, and is cornered by the cops.

Antiteater-X-Film. SCREENPLAY: Rainer Werner Fassbinder. CAMERA: Dietrich Lohmann. ASS'T CAMERA: Herbert Paetzold. EDITING: Thea Eymèsz. LIGHTING: Ekkehard Heinrich. ART DIRECTION: Kurt Raab and Rainer Werner Fassbinder. MUSIC: Peer Raben. MAKEUP: Sybille Danzer. ASS'T DIRECTOR: Kurt Raab. PROD'N MANAGERS: Peer Raben and Christian Hohoff.

With Karl Scheydt (Ricky), Elga Sorbas (Rosa), Jan George (Jan), Margarethe von Trotta (chambermaid), Ingrid Caven (singer), Ingeborg Scholz (Ricky's mother), Kurt Raab (Ricky's brother), Irm Hermann (whore), Ulli Lommel (gypsy), Rainer Werner Fassbinder (Franz).
Shot in Munich, August 1970. B/W, 35mm. 80 minutes.

1970
Pioniere in Ingolstadt
(Recruits in Ingolstadt)

Adapted from Marieluise Fleisser's 1929 play, which Brecht admired, and set in the present, Recruits in Ingolstadt concerns relationships between young military conscripts and the citizens, mainly young women, of Ingolstadt, a provincial town where the recruits have been sent to construct a wooden bridge. The disaffected soldiers have sex, drink, brutalize the mayor's effeminate son, and drown their field officer.

Janus Film und Fernsehen/Antiteater-X-Film, in association with Zweites Deutsches Fernsehen. SCREENPLAY: Rainer Werner Fassbinder, from the play by Marieluise Fleisser. CAMERA: Dietrich Lohmann. EDITING: Thea Eymèsz. ART DIRECTION: Kurt Raab. MUSIC: Peer Raben. ASS'T DIRECTOR: Gunter Krää.

With Hanna Schygulla (Berta), Harry Baer (Karl), Irm Hermann (Alma), Rudolf Waldemar Brem (Fabian), Klaus Löwitsch (field officer), Günther Kaufmann (Max), Carla Aulaulu (Frieda).
Shot in Landsberg am Lech and Munich, November 1970. Color, 35mm. 84 minutes.

Eddie Constantine, Hanna Schygulla

"It's true the film is about making a film, but the actual theme is how a group works and how leadership positions emerge and get worked out. And this theme, viewed objectively, is pretty important. To me it wasn't clear that it was a fresh start, but I knew that it had to be a conclusion. With this film we finally buried our first hope, namely the antiteater. I had no idea how things should go forward after that, but I knew that things couldn't continue as they were."

RWF, 1971

RWF, Kurt Raab, Ingeborg Scholz, Karl Scheydt

"*The American Soldier* . . . is a synthesis of *Love Is Colder than Death* and *Gods of the Plague*, and the narrative method is very concrete and professional. The earlier two films were actually accurate reconstructions of the people and atmosphere in Munich, while *The American Soldier* was more a real film and had a real story, and besides, it was larded with quotes from Hollywood films as well as French gangster films, and above all from the films of Raoul Walsh and John Huston."

RWF, 1971

Carla Aulaulu, Irm Hermann

1971

Händler der vier Jahreszeiten
(The Merchant of Four Seasons)

In 1950s Munich, Hans Epp, a former Foreign Legionnaire, upsets his bourgeois family by becoming a peddler of fruits and vegetables. He suffers a heart attack, and when he gets his health back, he takes on his old friend Harry as a partner. The business begins to do well, but the more he becomes a credit to his family, the more depressed he becomes. One sociable day he decides, while toasting everyone, to drink himself to death.

Tango-Film.
SCREENPLAY: Rainer Werner Fassbinder. **CAMERA:** Dietrich Lohmann. **ASS'T CAMERA:** Herbert Paetzold and Peter Gauhe. **EDITING:** Thea Eymèsz. **LIGHTING:** Ekkehard Heinrich. **ART DIRECTION:** Kurt Raab. **ASS'T DIRECTOR:** Harry Baer. **PROD'N MANAGERS:** Ingrid Fassbinder (i.e., Ingrid Caven), Christian Hohoff, and Karl Scheydt.

With Hans Hirschmüller (Hans Epp), Irm Hermann (Irmgard Epp), Hanna Schygulla (Hans's sister), Gusti Kreissl (mother), Kurt Raab (Schwager), Klaus Löwitsch (Harry), Ingrid Caven (woman at funeral).
Shot in Munich, August 1971. Color, 35mm. 89 minutes.

1972

Die bitteren Tränen der Petra von Kant
(The Bitter Tears of Petra von Kant)

At thirty-four, Petra von Kant is a successful fashion designer, divorced for three years, and living with Marlene, her assistant, who silently suffers Petra's domination of her. Petra falls in love with the young Karin and makes her a famous model. Wanting her freedom, Karin leaves Petra. Petra's daughter, Gabriele, and mother, Valerie, attend Petra's birthday party, and although Karin does not show up, Sidonie brings Petra a doll made to look like Karin.

Tango-Film.
SCREENPLAY: Rainer Werner Fassbinder, from his play. **CAMERA:** Michael Ballhaus. **EDITING:** Thea Eymèsz. **ART DIRECTION:** Kurt Raab. **SOUND:** Gunther Kortwich. **MAKEUP:** Sybille Danzer. **ASS'T DIRECTORS:** Harry Baer and Kurt Raab.

With Margit Carstensen (Petra von Kant), Hanna Schygulla (Karin Thimm), Irm Hermann (Marlene), Eva Mattes (Gabriele von Kant), Katrin Schaake (Sidonie von Grasenabb), Gisela Fackeldey (Valerie von Kant).
Shot in Worpswede, January 1972. Color, 35mm. 124 minutes.

1972

Wildwechsel
(Jail Bait)

Sexually precocious and spoiled, fourteen-year-old Hanni, the only child of a pious couple, allows herself to be seduced by nineteen-year-old Franz. When their affair becomes known, he is imprisoned on a morals charge. They resume the relationship when he is released, and she becomes pregnant. To avoid getting her father's permission for an abortion, she suggests that Franz murder him at a game pass ("Wildwechsel"), a tower in the woods from which wild animals may be watched.

Intertel, in association with Sender Freies Berlin.
SCREENPLAY: Rainer Werner Fassbinder, from the play by Franz Xaver Kroetz. **CAMERA:** Dietrich Lohmann. **EDITING:** Thea Eymèsz. **ART DIRECTION:** Kurt Raab.

With Eva Mattes (Hanni), Jörg von Liebenfels (Erwin), Ruth Drexel (Hilda), Harry Baer (Franz), Rudolf Waldemar Brem (Dieter), Hanna Schygulla (doctor), Kurt Raab (chef).
Shot in Straubing and vicinity, March 1972. Color, 35mm. 102 minutes.

"*The Merchant* comes from a period in which I had gotten intensely involved with the melodramas of Douglas Sirk and had learned a couple of things from them; I had figured out that the public likes them and is interested in them, to put it simply. For example, the story with Karl Scheydt [who plays Anzell in the film], where he spends the night with the wife of the fruit seller and then later comes in again as an employee. Previously I would not actually have done that, because to me that would have been too much like something in a dream. And suddenly I began trusting myself."

RWF, 1973

Hans Hirschmüller

Hanna Schygulla, Margit Carstensen

"Marlene leaves because she had accepted her role as the oppressed and exploited one and because in reality she is frightened by the freedom offered to her. Freedom means, specifically, having to think about her life, and she isn't used to that. She had always acted like a commando and never made her own decisions. So freedom scared her, and when she finally abandons Petra, she doesn't go towards freedom, in my opinion, but in search of another position as slave."

RWF, 1973

The charge is made against you from time to time that your films are a denunciation of humanity.
"I would defend myself against a charge of denigrating people in anything I've made. On the contrary, I think that I really put people down less than just about anyone and a lot of the time approach people too positively, to the point where it almost can't be justified. Like in *Jail Bait*, when the father tells about his war experiences, when his opinions are particularly horrible, we always deal with them very sensitively, in order to be clear that what's horrible is what they're saying and . . . not what they are."

1972

Acht Stunden sind kein Tag
(Eight Hours Don't Make a Day)

This popular television series is about a working-class family, the Krugers in Cologne, headed by a sixty-year-old widow, Oma. Alternating between domestic drama and personal romance on the one hand and issues of the workplace and housing on the other, the series takes the position that most problems are surmountable through solidarity. It was conceived as an eight-part television series but only five of the scripts written for the program were shot.

Westdeutscher Rundfunk.
TELEPLAY: Rainer Werner Fassbinder. CAMERA: Dietrich Lohmann. EDITING: Marie-Anne Gerhardt. ART DIRECTION: Kurt Raab. MUSIC: Jean Gepoint (i.e., Jens Wilhelm Petersen). ASS'T DIRECTORS: Renate Leiffer and Eberhard Schubert.

With Gottfried John (Jochen), Hanna Schygulla (Marion), Luise Ullrich (Oma), Werner Finck (Gregor), Anita Bucher (Käthe), Wolfried Lier (Wolf), Christine Oesterlein (Klara), Kurt Raab (Harald), Renate Roland (Monika), Irm Hermann (Irmgard Erlkönig), Rudolf Waldemar Brem (Rolf), Wolfgang Schenck (Franz), Peter Gauhe (Ernst).
Shot in Cologne, April–August 1972. Color, 16mm. Episode one: "Jochen und Marion," 101 minutes; episode two: "Oma und Gregor," 99 minutes; episode three: "Franz und Ernst," 92 minutes; episode four: "Harald und Monika," 89 minutes; episode five: "Irmgard und Rolf," 89 minutes.

1972

Bremer Freiheit
(Bremen Freedom)

Suggested by an early-nineteenth-century case in the Bremen court archives, the film tells of a Bremen housewife and mother, Geesche, who poisoned her abusive husband Miltenberger and then took matters further.

Telefilm Saar, in association with Saarländischer Rundfunk.
TELEPLAY: Rainer Werner Fassbinder and Dietrich Lohmann, from the stage play by Fassbinder. CAMERA: Dietrich Lohmann, Hans Schugg, and Peter Weyrich. EDITING: Friedrich Niquet and Monika Solzbacher. ART DIRECTION: Kurt Raab. ASS'T DIRECTOR: Fritz Müller-Scherz.

With Margit Carstensen (Geesche), Ulli Lommel (Miltenberger), Wolfgang Schenck (Gottfried), Walter Sedlmayr (vicar), Wolfgang Kieling (Timm), Kurt Raab (Zimmerman), Hanna Schygulla (Luise Maurer), Lilo Pempeit (mother), Rainer Werner Fassbinder (Rumpf).
Shot in Saarbrücken (studio), September 1972. Color, video. 87 minutes.

1973

Welt am Draht
(World on a Wire)

In the Institute for Cybernetics and Futurology, the computer Simulacron creates a virtual future, which may be viewed on a monitor. All seems well until Vollmer, the director of the Institute, commits suicide. His successor Stiller is not convinced of Vollmer's death, and the researchers, including Vollmer's daughter, begin to realize that they themselves may be artificial, controlled by an unperceived intelligence.

Westdeutsche Rundfunk.
TELEPLAY: Fritz Müller-Scherz and Rainer Werner Fassbinder, from the novel by Daniel F. Galouyé. CAMERA: Michael Ballhaus. EDITING: Marie-Anne Gerhardt. ART DIRECTION: Kurt Raab. MUSIC: Gottfried Hüngsberg. ASS'T DIRECTORS: Renate Leiffer and Fritz Müller-Scherz.

With Klaus Löwitsch (Fred Stiller), Mascha Elm Rabben (Eva), Adrian Hoven (Vollmer), Ivan Desny (Lause), Günter Lamprecht (Wolfgang), Margit Carstensen (Schmidt-Gentner), Kurt Raab (Holm), Ulli Lommel (Rupp).
Shot in Cologne, Munich, and Paris, January–March 1973. Color, 16mm. Part one: 99 minutes; part two: 106 minutes.

Gottfried John

"It is above all a matter of the cohesion and solidarity of workers. Since the employer treats the worker as an isolated person, it's difficult for them to show solidarity. We have tried to say: unity means strength. And we've documented that in various examples. We show that there exists for workers the possibility of defending themselves, and that they can best do this in a group."

RWF, 1973

Margit Carstensen

"When both Geesche [in *Bremen Freedom*] and Whity [in *Whity*] die, it really comes from the attempt of the oppressed to defend themselves. It's just not the right way, and here you have to put in an explanation, you have to show people how they can put up resistance without ending up in the desert."

RWF, 1973

"I directed a series of two one-and-a-half-hour segments based on a novel by Daniel F. Galouyé. It's a very beautiful story called *World on a Wire* that depicts a world where one is able to make projections of people with a computer. And of course that leads to the uncertainty of whether someone is himself a projection, since in this virtual world the projections resemble reality. Perhaps another larger world made us as a virtual one? In this sense it deals with an old philosophical model, which here takes on a certain horror."

RWF, 1973

Kurt Raab

1973
Nora Helmer

To help her critically ill husband Torvald, and without his knowledge, Nora Helmer borrows from the crafty Krogsted but falsifies her father's signature on the security note.

Telefilm Saar, in association with Saarländischer Rundfunk.
TELEPLAY: Adapted from Henrik Ibsen's *A Doll's House*, translated by Bernhard Schulze. **CAMERA:** Willi Raber, Wilfried Mier, Peter Weyrich, Gisela Loew, and Hans Schugg. **EDITING:** Anne-Marie Bornheimer and Friedrich Niquet. **ART DIRECTION:** Friedhelm Boehm. **COSTUMES:** Barbara Baum. **ASS'T DIRECTORS:** Fritz Müller-Scherz and Rainer Langhans.

With Margit Carstensen (Nora), Joachim Hansen (Torvald), Barbara Valentin (Frau Linde), Ulli Lommel (Krogsted), Klaus Löwitsch (Dr. Rank), Lilo Pempeit (Marie), Irm Hermann (Helene).
Shot in Saarbrücken (studio), May 1973. Color, video. 101 minutes.

1973
Angst essen Seele auf
(Ali: Fear Eats the Soul)

In a pub frequented by foreign workers, Emmi Kurowski, a widowed cleaning woman, meets Ali, a Moroccan, about twenty years her junior. They dance, and she invites him home. Lonely and wanting companionship, they marry. Emmi's children are outraged and Ali's friends ridicule him for marrying "a grandmother." They go on a trip, hoping everything will be better when they return. It is, but without prejudice to bind them together from the outside, their relationship begins to unravel.

Tango-Film.
SCREENPLAY: Rainer Werner Fassbinder. **CAMERA:** Jürgen Jürges. **ASS'T CAMERA:** Thomas Schwan. **EDITING:** Thea Eymèsz. **LIGHTING:** Ekkehard Heinrich. **ART DIRECTION:** Rainer Werner Fassbinder. **MAKEUP:** Helga Kempke. **SOUND:** Fritz Müller-Scherz. **ASS'T DIRECTOR:** Rainer Langhans.

With Brigitte Mira (Emmi), El Hedi ben Salem (Ali), Barbara Valentin (owner of bar), Irm Hermann (Krista), Rainer Werner Fassbinder (Eugen), Karl Scheydt (Albert), Liselotte Eder (Mrs. Münchmeyer), Hark Bohm (doctor).
Shot in Munich, September 1973. Color, 35mm. 93 minutes.

1973
Martha

Thirty-year-old Martha Hyer, self-absorbed and single, lives with her parents and works in a library. Her father dies while vacationing with her in Rome, and at the German Embassy she encounters Helmut Salomon, whom she meets again in Germany. She decides to marry him, and although he is not particularly attracted to her, he agrees. After a peculiar honeymoon, he moves Martha to a house he has bought outside of town, and there he slowly instills fear in her and comes to dominate her.

Westdeutscher Rundfunk/Pro-ject Filmproduktion im Filmverlag der Autoren.
PRODUCER: Peter Märthesheimer. **TELEPLAY:** Rainer Werner Fassbinder, based on a novel by Cornell Woolrich. **CAMERA:** Michael Ballhaus. **EDITING:** Liesgret Schmitt-Klink. **ART DIRECTION:** Kurt Raab. **SOUND:** Manfred Oelschlegel. **ASS'T DIRECTORS:** Fritz Müller-Scherz and Renate Leiffer.

With Margit Carstensen (Martha), Karlheinz Böhm (Helmut), Gisela Fackeldey (mother), Adrian Hoven (father), Barbara Valentin (Marianne), Ingrid Caven (Ilse).
Shot in Konstanz, Ottobeuren, Kreuzlingen, Rome, and S. Felice Zirceo, July–September 1973. Color, 16mm. 112 minutes.

Have you altered anything in the play?

"We haven't changed anything, just cut quite a bit. In our version, for example, Nora doesn't go away at the end. She stays, since in ten thousand families there's the same blowout between Nora and Helmer, and usually the woman doesn't leave, even when she probably should. In fact she has no other options, and so people always find some way to accommodate themselves, which in the end is even more horrible. "

RWF, 1973

Joachim Hansen, Margit Carstensen

"I had already used the story in a film once, it was actually in *The American Soldier*, where it was told by a barmaid, in a long sequence where the girl sits on a bed. It's about an old German woman who is around sixty and a young Turkish guest worker. They marry and one day she is murdered. Nobody knows who the killer is—whether it was her husband or one of his Turkish pals. But I didn't want to tell the story the way it actually happened. I wanted to give the young Turk and the old woman the chance to live together. . . ."

RWF, 1973

Brigitte Mira, El Hedi ben Salem

"Of the films I've made with Fassbinder up to now, I like *Martha* best. For *Martha* we had, by Fassbinder's stan- dards, a lot of time: twenty-six shooting days. Fassbinder wanted me to photograph the entire film with one lens, without zoom. We maintained this principle with a few exceptions, and this was after we had just exploited the full range of technical possibilities doing *World on a Wire*. This restriction led to new ways of thinking about things and fresh experiments, and I noticed that because it was photographed this way, the film attained a strength and consistency that we wouldn't have been able to achieve otherwise."

Michael Ballhaus, 1974

Margit Carstensen

1972/74
Fontane Effi Briest
(Effi Briest)

In the 1890s, seventeen-year-old Effi Briest lives a privileged life outside Berlin. She and her ambitious parents are honored when Baron von Instetten, twenty years older than Effi, asks to marry her. The Baron and Effi settle in a small community where she is regarded as an outsider. She allows herself to be courted by Major Crampas, a young bachelor. Effi and her husband later move to Berlin, where the Baron finds old letters from the Major. Fassbinder added a subtitle: "Effi Briest, or Many who have an idea of their possibilities and needs nevertheless accept the prevailing order in the way they act, and thereby strengthen and comfirm it absolutely."

Tango-Film, Munich. **SCREENPLAY:** Rainer Werner Fassbinder, from the 1894 novel by Theodor Fontane. **CAMERA:** Dietrich Lohmann and Jürgen Jürges. **ASS'T CAMERA:** Thomas Schwan and Herbert Paetzold. **EDITING:** Thea Eymèsz. **LIGHTING:** Ernst Küsters and Ekkehard Heinrich. **ART DIRECTION:** Kurt Raab. **COSTUMES:** Barbara Baum. **MAKEUP:** Sybille Danzer. **SOUND:** Fritz Müller-Scherz. **ASS'T DIRECTORS:** Rainer Langhans and Fritz Müller-Scherz.

With Hanna Schygulla (Effi), Wolfgang Schenck (Baron Geert von Instetten), Karlheinz Böhm (councilman Wüllersdorf), Ulli Lommel (Major Crampas), Ursula Strätz (Roswitha), Irm Hermann (Johanna), Lilo Pempeit (Effi's mother), Herbert Steinmetz (Effi's father), Hark Bohm (druggist). Narrated by Rainer Werner Fassbinder.
Shot in Munich, Vienna, Aeroskobing (Denmark), Schleswig-Holstein, and the Black Forest, September–October 1972/October–November 1973. B/W, 35mm. 141 minutes.

1974
Faustrecht der Freiheit
(Fox and His Friends)

Franz Biberkopf, a guileless young fellow known as Fox, loses his job in a traveling freak show, but he wins half a million marks in the lottery. Used to hustling older men in public toilets, Fox meets Max, a dapper antique dealer, who introduces Max to Eugen, a handsome but vulpine sophisticate. Fox seduces Eugen, but Eugen uses Fox's winnings to help his father's troubled business and to decorate his apartment. The film is dedicated to "Armin and the others."

Tango-Film, Munich/City Film GmbH, Berlin. **PRODUCER:** Christian Hohoff. **SCREENPLAY:** Rainer Werner Fassbinder and Christian Hohoff. **CAMERA:** Michael Ballhaus. **EDITING:** Thea Eymèsz. **ART DIRECTION:** Kurt Raab. **MUSIC:** Peer Raben. **COSTUMES:** Helga Kempke. **ASS'T DIRECTOR:** Irm Hermann.

With Rainer Werner Fassbinder (Franz Biberkopf), Peter Chatel (Eugen), Karlheinz Böhm (Max), Rudolf Lenz (Rechtsanwalt), Karl Scheydt (Klaus), Hans Zander (Springer), Kurt Raab (Vodka Peter), Irm Hermann (Madame Cherie).
Shot in Marrakech and Munich, April and July 1974. Color, 35mm. 123 minutes.

1974
Wie ein Vogel auf dem Draht
(Like a Bird on a Wire)

A pseudo variety show about the Aufbau-Ära, the time of the German "economic miracle," when Konrad Adenauer was Chancellor of the Federal Republic of Germany (1949–63). Songs are sung and Brigitte Mira tells a few jokes.

Westdeutscher Rundfunk. **TELEPLAY:** Rainer Werner Fassbinder and Christian Hohoff. **CAMERA:** Erhard Spandel. **ART DIRECTION:** Kurt Raab. **MUSICAL ADAPTATION:** Ingfried Hoffmann. **LYRICS:** Anja Hauptmann. **ORCHESTRA CONDUCTOR:** Kurt Edelhagan.

With Brigitte Mira, Evelyn Künneke.
Shot in Cologne, July 1974. Color, video. 44 minutes.

"It seems to me that one does not experience the film in the same way as other films that affect the heart or the emotions; instead, it is an attempt to make a film entirely for the head, a film, that is, in which one doesn't give up thinking but instead begins to think, and just as in reading one really makes sense of letters and sentences only through imagination, so it should also happen in this film. Thus everyone should have the possibility and the freedom to make this film his own, as he sees it."

RWF, 1974

Ulli Lommel, Hanna Schygulla

Peter Chatel, RWF

"I think it's incidental and beside the point that the story has to do with gays. It could just as well take place among other people. I even think that people pay more attention to the details for this reason, because if it were only a 'normal love story,' the melodramatic aspect would be a lot stronger."

RWF, 1974

"*Like a Bird on a Wire* is an attempt to do a show about the Adenauer era. For us it certainly wasn't entirely successful. But the film does reveal the utter repulsiveness and sentimentality of that time."

RWF, 1975

1975

Mutter Küsters' Fahrt zum Himmel
(Mother Küsters Goes to Heaven)

Emma Küsters, a Frankfurt housewife, shares her modest apartment with her son Ernst and his pregnant wife Helene. A factory employee who goes berserk due to imminent layoffs, killing the plant owner's son and committing suicide, turns out to have been Emma's husband. The family is besieged by reporters, Emma's son and daughter-in-law leave for Finland, and her other daughter, the chanteuse Corinna, uses her father's notoriety to further her career. To clear her husband's name, Emma takes up with a Communist couple and then turns to an anarchist group.

Tango-Film, Munich.
SCREENPLAY: Rainer Werner Fassbinder with Kurt Raab. **CAMERA:** Michael Ballhaus. **ASS'T CAMERA:** Thomas Schwan. **EDITING:** Thea Eymèsz. **ART DIRECTION:** Kurt Raab. **SOUND:** Wolfgang Hoffmann. **MUSIC:** Peer Raben. **ASS'T DIRECTOR:** Renate Leiffer. **PROD'N MANAGER:** Christian Hohoff.

With Brigitte Mira (Emma Küsters), Ingrid Caven (Corinna), Karlheinz Böhm (Tillmann), Margit Carstensen (Frau Tillmann), Irm Hermann (Helene), Armin Meier (Ernst), Gottfried John (the journalist Niemeyer).
Shot in Frankfurt, February–March 1975. Color, 35mm. Note: Two versions of the film were distributed, one in the United States (the "happy" ending, as originally written by Fassbinder), the other in Germany (the "radical" ending, as originally shot by Fassbinder). 120 minutes.

1975

Angst vor der Angst
(Fear of Fear)

Margot Staudte, a housewife living comfortably, loves her husband Kurt and daughter Bibi. Her in-laws are interfering but tolerable. Toward the end of her second pregnancy, undirected fear begins to permeate her. Her anxiety grows. After she gives birth to a son, alcohol and drugs temporarily calm but do not diminish her terror.

Westdeutscher Rundfunk.
PRODUCER: Peter Märthesheimer. **TELEPLAY:** Rainer Werner Fassbinder, from an idea by Asta Scheib. **CAMERA:** Jürgen Jürges and Ulrich Prinz. **EDITING:** Liesgret Schmitt-Klink and Beate Fischer-Weiskirch. **ART DIRECTION:** Kurt Raab. **SOUND:** Manfred Oelschlegel and Hans Pampuch. **MUSIC:** Peer Raben. **ASS'T DIRECTOR:** Renate Leiffer.

With Margit Carstensen (Margot), Ulrich Faulhaber (Kurt), Brigitte Mira (Kurt's mother), Irm Hermann (Lore), Armin Meier (Karli), Adrian Hoven (Dr. Merck), Ingrid Caven (Edda).
Shot in Cologne and Bonn, April–May 1975. Color, 16mm. 88 minutes.

1975

Ich will doch nur, dass Ihr mich liebt
(I Only Want You to Love Me)

Peter, a young man, is serving ten years for the seemingly unmotivated murder of a cafe owner. A prison psychiatrist probes Peter's past and learns that his hardworking parents were strict disciplinarians who criticized and punished Peter but gave him no encouragement or love. Having married his sweetheart Elke, Peter moved to Munich where he found work. Believing mistakenly that Elke's love was predicated on his gifts to her, Peter went seriously and secretly into debt. They had a baby, and an anticipated raise did not materialize.

Bavaria Atelier in association with Westdeutscher Rundfunk.
PRODUCER: Peter Märthesheimer. **SCREENPLAY:** Rainer Werner Fassbinder, from an interview in the book *Lebenslänglich* by Klaus Antes and Christiane Erhardt. **CAMERA:** Michael Ballhaus. **EDITING:** Liesgret Schmitt-Klink. **ART DIRECTION:** Kurt Raab. **SOUND:** Karsten Ullrich. **MUSIC:** Peer Raben. **MAKEUP:** Peter Knöpfle and Elke Müller. **ASS'T DIRECTORS:** Renate Leiffer and Christian Hohoff.

With Vitus Zeplichal (Peter), Elke Aberle (Erika), Alexander Allerson (father), Ernie Mangold (mother), Johanna Hofer (grandmother), Katharina Buchhammer (Ulla), Armin Meier (Polier), Erika Runge (interviewer).
Shot in Munich and vicinity, November–December 1975. Color, 16mm. 104 minutes.

Gottfried John, Brigitte Mira

Margit Carstensen, Adrian Hoven

"As it happens, the adolescence of our Peter actually coincides with a very important development in this society, the so-called Economic Miracle. It isn't dealt with explicitly in the film . . . but when I think of the kind of childhood Peter has endured, it plays an important role. At that time the grown-ups were busy with what they called 'construction,' and one could already imagine that their children became an afterthought and that not very much time was left over to 'construct' them as well. Anyway, I know an awful lot of people who were raised at that time or around then, and they are what we call today 'difficult,' and sometimes they're just nuts."

RWF, 1976

Vitus Zeplichal, Elke Aberle

1976

Satansbraten
(Satan's Brew)

During the "revolution of 1968," writer Walter Kranz became a minor celebrity. Now he has an enormous writer's block, but as his haranguing wife Luise reminds him, the rent must be paid on the apartment they share with Ernst, Walter's idiot brother, who torments flies and bothers visiting women like Andrée, a librarian who admires Walter. Walter thinks he will make some money interviewing a prostitute, but Luise finds him quoting the poet Stefan George. Walter believes himself to be George's reincarnation, and life at the Kranzes' becomes increasingly hysterical.

Albatros Produktion/Tango-Film.
PRODUCER: Michael Fengler. **SCREENPLAY:** Rainer Werner Fassbinder. **CAMERA:** Jürgen Jürges and Michael Ballhaus. **EDITING:** Thea Eymèsz and Gabi Eichel. **ART DIRECTION:** Kurt Raab and Ulrike Bode. **SOUND:** Paul Schöler, Rolf-Peter Notz, and Roland Henschke. **MUSIC:** Peer Raben. **MAKEUP:** Evelyn Döhring and Jo Baum. **ASS'T DIRECTORS:** Ila von Hasperg, Christa Reeh, and Renate Leiffer.

With Kurt Raab (Walter Kranz), Margit Carstensen (Andrée), Helen Vita (Luise Kranz), Volker Spengler (Ernst), Ingrid Caven (Lilly), Marquard Bohm (Rolf), Ulli Lommel (Lauf).
Shot in Munich, January–February 1976. Color, 35mm. 113 minutes.

1976

Chinesisches Roulette
(Chinese Roulette)

The crippled, mean-spirited Angela invites her estranged parents, whose infidelities she blames for her infirmity, up from Munich for a weekend at the family's country estate. The parents, Ariane and Gerhard, unaware that the other has been invited, bring their respective lovers, Kolbe and Irene. Adding to the mix is Angela's faithful mute governess, Traunitz, and Kast the housekeeper and her poet son, Gabriel. A nasty truth-game, Chinese Roulette, is played after dinner, and a shot rings out.

Albatros Produktion/Les Films du Losange.
PRODUCER: Michael Fengler. **SCREENPLAY:** Rainer Werner Fassbinder. **CAMERA:** Michael Ballhaus. **EDITING:** Ila von Hasperg and Juliane Lorenz. **ART DIRECTION:** Curd Melber. **SOUND:** Roland Henschke. **MUSIC:** Peer Raben. **MAKEUP:** Jo Braun. **ASS'T DIRECTOR:** Ila von Hasperg.

With Margit Carstensen (Ariane), Anna Karina (Irene), Alexander Allerson (Gerhard), Ulli Lommel (Kolbe), Andrea Schober (Angela), Macha Meril (Traunitz), Brigitte Mira (Kast), Volker Spengler (Gabriel), Armin Meier (Tankwart).
Shot in Stöckach and vicinity, and Munich, April–June 1976. Color, 35mm. 86 minutes.

1977/83

Bolwieser
(The Stationmaster's Wife)

Bolwieser is stationmaster in the Bavarian town of Werburg in the late 1920s. His slavish passion for his wife Hanni, daughter of a wealthy brewer, does not satisfy her. She begins a liaison with Franz Merkl, a crafty butcher to whom she loans money to buy a pub. The town gossips but Bolwieser seems oblivious to Hanni's philandering. When Hanni and Franz sue the gossips, Bolwieser is the principal witness. When Hanni switches her affections to the hairdresser Schaftaller, Franz seeks revenge by having Bolwieser indicted for perjury. Note: The stationmaster (Bolwieser) was the focus of the original television production; in the theatrical release, edited from the television film, the stationmaster's wife has become the principal character.

Bavaria Atelier in association with Zweites Deutsches Fernsehen.
SCREENPLAY: Rainer Werner Fassbinder, from the novel by Oskar Maria Graf. **CAMERA:** Michael Ballhaus. **ASS'T CAMERA:** Horst Knechtal. **EDITING:** Ila von Hasperg and Juliane Lorenz (television version); Rainer Werner Fassbinder (theatrical version). **ART DIRECTION:** Kurt Raab, Nico Kehrhan, and Peter Müller. **COSTUMES:** Monika Altmann-Kriger. **SOUND:** Reinhard Gloge, Klaus Maier, Hans-Joachim Richter, and Werner Bohm. **MUSIC:** Peer Raben. **ASS'T DIRECTORS:** Christian Hohoff, Ila von Hasperg, and Udo Kier.

With Kurt Raab (Xaver Ferdinand Maria Bolwieser), Elisabeth Trissenaar (Hanni), Bernhard Helfrich (Franz Merkl), Udo Kier (Schafftaler), Volker Spengler (Mangst), Armin Meier (Scherber), Liselotte Pempeit (Mrs. Käser), Gustl Bayrhammer (Hanni's father), Peter Kern (Treuberger).
Shot in Maxgrün, Förmitzsee, Bayreuth, Hof, and Munich, October–December 1976. Color, 16mm (television); 35mm (theatrical, 1983). Part one: 104 minutes; part two: 96 minutes (television). 112 minutes (theatrical).

"This is an experiment that has to do with a lot of totally personal things that I've been involved with, that has something to do with my attitude when I read the newspaper, how I react to certain things, or when I'm talking to people who go on as if it were still 1968, and what happened to me then, the kinds of aggression that I vented then . . . and that are still coming out of me and how I am still trying to overcome that, because I tell myself, that is still the right way. Out of this complete muddle of feelings and thoughts I try to tell a clear story."

RWF, 1976

Volker Spengler

"I have tried to make a film that pushes artificiality, an artificial form, to extremes in order to be able to totally call it into question. I'm pretty certain that in film history there is no single film that contains so many camera movements, traveling shots, and counter-movements of the actors. The film I've made, which appears to speak out for marriage as an institution, is in reality about how infamous, mendacious, and destructive marriages are, and perhaps, precisely because of this equivocation, it becomes stronger than other films that explicitly speak out against marriage."

RWF, 1977

Ulli Lommel, Alexander Allerson

Elisabeth Trissenaar, Kurt Raab

1977
Frauen in New York
(Women in New York)

In 1930s Manhattan a circle of wives with the leisure to lunch is threatened when one of them, Mary, learns that her husband has a mistress, Miss Chrystal Allen. The film is a staging for television of the Rainer Werner Fassbinder production of Clare Boothe Luce's 1936 play at the Deutsches Schauspielhaus in Hamburg.

Norddeutscher Rundfunk.
SCREENPLAY: Translated by Nora Gray from Clare Boothe Luce's play *The Women*. **CAMERA:** Michael Ballhaus. **EDITING:** Wolfgang Kerhutt. **ART DIRECTION:** Rolf Glittenberg. **COSTUMES:** Frieda Parmeggiani. **SOUND:** Horst Faahs.

With Christa Berndl (Mary, Mrs. Stephen Haines), Margit Carstensen (Sylvia, Mrs. Harold Fowler), Anne-Marie Kuster (Peggy, Mrs. John Day), Eva Mattes (Edith, Mrs. Phelps Porter), Barbara Sukowa (Chrystal Allen).
Shot in Hamburg, March 1977. Color, 16mm.
111 minutes.

1977
Despair — Eine Reise ins Licht
(Despair)

In early 1930s Berlin, Hermann, a Russian exile, owns a small, insolvent chocolate factory. His wife, the vulgar Lydia, adores her cousin, the penniless artist Ardalion. Hermann thinks of himself as literally outside himself, and for instance sees himself making love to Lydia. He comes across Felix, whom he believes to be his double, and conspires to murder Felix and collect his own life insurance. Hermann's increasing madness reflects the growing insanity of the world outside as the Nazis come to power. The film is dedicated to "Antonin Artaud, Vincent van Gogh, Unica Zürn."

NF Geria II/Westdeutscher Rundfunk.
PRODUCER: Lutz Hengst. **SCREENPLAY:** Tom Stoppard, from the novel by Vladimir Nabokov. **CAMERA:** Michael Ballhaus. **ASS'T CAMERA:** Horst Knechtel and Otto Kirchhoff. **EDITING:** Juliane Lorenz and *Franz Walsch* (i.e., Rainer Werner Fassbinder). **PROD'N DESIGNER:** Rolf Zehetbauer. **ART DIRECTION:** Herbert Strabel and Jochen Schumacher. **COSTUMES:** Dagmar Schauberger. **MAKEUP:** Peter Knöpfle and Anni Nöbauer. **SOUND:** James Willis and Milan Bor. **MUSIC:** Peer Raben. **ASS'T DIRECTORS:** Harry Baer and Stefan Zurcher. **PROD'N MANAGER:** Dieter Minx.

With Dirk Bogarde (Hermann Hermann), Andrea Ferréol (Lydia), Volker Spengler (Ardalion), Klaus Löwitsch (Felix), Alexander Allerson (Mayer), Bernhard Wicki (Orlovius), Peter Kern (Müller), Gottfried John (Perebrodov), Hark Bohm (doctor), Liselotte Eder (secretary), Armin Meier (foreman), Ingrid Caven (hotel employee).
Shot in Munich, Interlaken, Berlin, Lübeck, Braunschweig, Hamburg, and Mölln. Color, 35mm.
119 minutes.

1978
Episode of *Deutschland im Herbst*
(Germany in Autumn)

Thirteen German writers and directors conceived this collective work in response to the deaths in the fall of 1977 of Hans-Martin Schleyer, an executive kidnapped and killed by political terrorists, and the subsequent "suicides" of the last three members of the notorious Baader-Meinhof revolutionary group. Fassbinder's episode concerns a radical filmmaker, Rainer Werner Fassbinder, who finds German complacency too much to bear. He hectors his mother into taking a stand on terrorism, and argues with his lover, a foreign worker who supports the state position on terrorism.

Pro-ject Filmproduktion im Filmverlag der Autoren/ Hallelujah-Film/Kairos-Film.
PRODUCERS: Theo Hinz and Eberhard Junkersdorf. **SCREENPLAY:** Rainer Werner Fassbinder. **CAMERA:** Michael Ballhaus. **EDITING:** Juliane Lorenz. **SOUND:** Roland Henschke.

With Rainer Werner Fassbinder, Liselotte Eder, Armin Meier.
Shot in Munich, October 1977. Color, 35mm.
26 minutes.

Barbara Sukowa, Margit Carstensen

"I take women more seriously than directors usually do. To my mind, women don't exist to turn men on. They don't have this function of merely being objects. In fact, that is one aspect of the cinema I really despise. And I want to show that women, more than men, are obliged to resort to underhanded methods to avoid being mere objects."

RWF, 1976

Volker Spengler, Dirk Bogarde, Andrea Ferréol

"What do people such as Hermann Hermann usually do if it becomes clear to them that they are standing at a turning point where they have every-thing behind them and nothing ahead of them? They back off, they knuckle under, and before they acknowledge that their life is at an end, they spend what remains of it in a sea of compro-mises and self-denial. The few, on the other hand, who rebel, if perhaps in totally irrational ways, who reach for something, discover something further that gives them hope."

RWF, 1977

RWF

"The problem is really just that we don't have a censor. If we had one, we would know what we can and what we can't do, and then we would also know under what circumstances we could fight. There is nothing that one could accurately call a censor—I would describe it more as a climate in which from time to time something . . . now, it isn't forbidden, but we say: that won't be possible."

RWF, 1978

1978

Die Ehe der Maria Braun
(The Marriage of Maria Braun)

In Germany toward World War II's end, as bombs interrupt the ceremony, Maria and Private Hermann Braun are married. After being sent to the Russian front, Hermann is reported missing. Although Maria believes he is alive, her brother-in-law, just returned from a prisoner-of-war camp in Russia, confirms his death. Maria meets a black GI, Bill, begins an affair, and becomes pregnant. Hermann suddenly returns at an inopportune moment. Bill is killed and Hermann is sent to prison. While Maria waits earnestly for Hermann, she participates wholeheartedly in the German Economic Miracle. The film is dedicated to Peter Zadek.

Albatros Produktion/Trio-Film/Tango-Film/Westdeutscher Rundfunk.
PRODUCER: Michael Fengler. **SCREENPLAY:** Peter Märtesheimer and Pea Fröhlich, from an idea by Rainer Werner Fassbinder. **CAMERA:** Michael Ballhaus. **ASS'T CAMERA:** Horst Knechtel. **EDITORS:** *Franz Walsch* (i.e., Rainer Werner Fassbinder) and Juliane Lorenz. **ART DIRECTION:** Norbert Scherer and Helga Ballhaus. **COSTUMES:** Barbara Baum. **MAKEUP:** Anni Nöbauer. **SOUND:** Jim Willis. **MUSIC:** Peer Raben. **ASS'T DIRECTOR:** Rolf Bührmann. **PROD'N MANAGERS:** Martin Häussler and Harry Zöttl.

With Hanna Schygulla (Maria), Klaus Löwitsch (Hermann), Ivan Desny (Oswald), Gottfried John (Willi), Gisela Uhlen (mother), Günter Lamprecht (Wetzel), Elisabeth Trissenaar (Betti), Liselotte Eder (Mrs. Ehmke), Hark Bohm (Senkenberg), Volker Spengler (Schaffner), Michael Ballhaus (lawyer), Rainer Werner Fassbinder (black-marketeer).
Shot in Coburg and Berlin, January–March 1978. Color, 35mm. 120 minutes.

1978

In einem Jahr mit 13 Monden
(In a Year of 13 Moons)

The film follows the last five days of transsexual Elvira Weishaupt, born Erwin, unwanted and raised by nuns. Married and working as a butcher, Erwin fell in love with Anton, who said offhandedly, "Too bad you're not a girl." After having his sex changed, Erwin returned to Frankfurt as Elvira and suffered one rejection after another. In the company of the sweet-natured whore Zora, Elvira sets out to revisit the stations of his life as a man.

Tango-Film/Pro-ject Filmproduktion im Filmverlag der Autoren.
SCREENPLAY, CAMERA, EDITING, AND ART DIRECTION: Rainer Werner Fassbinder. **EDITING:** Juliane Lorenz. **ASS'T CAMERA:** Werner Lüring. **SOUND:** Karl Scheydt and Wolfgang Mund. **MUSIC:** Suicide, Roxy Music, and Peer Raben.

With Volker Spengler (Elvira Weishaupt), Ingrid Caven (Zora), Karl Scheydt (Christoph Hacker), Gottfried John (Anton Seitz), Elisabeth Trissenaar (Irene Weishaupt), Eva Mattes (Marie-Ann Weishaupt), Günther Kaufmann (bouncer), Liselotte Eder (Sister Gudrun), Walter Bockmayer (Seelen-Frieda).
Shot in Frankfurt, July–August 1978. Color, 35mm. 124 minutes.

1978/79

Die dritte Generation
(The Third Generation)

In West Berlin in 1978, the computer magnate P. J. Lurz seeks to increase sales by covertly promoting terrorism. He hires August, who recruits a "third generation" of terrorists, middle-class people for whom terrorism has become a lifestyle. The film is dedicated to "Someone who is a true lover, and that is probably no one." However, when asked about this dedication, Juliane Lorenz, the film's editor, said that she misread Fassbinder's notes, and what he wrote was that the film was to be dedicated to "Someone who is a true liberal. . . ." Fassbinder, who saw the film and read the dedication on screen, never mentioned the error to Lorenz.

Tango-Film/Pro-ject Filmproduktion im Filmverlag der Autoren.
SCREENPLAY AND CAMERA: Rainer Werner Fassbinder. **ASS'T CAMERA:** Hans-Günther Bücking and Alexander Witt. **EDITING:** Juliane Lorenz. **ASS'T EDITOR:** Karin Viesel. **LIGHTING:** Ekkehard Heinrich. **ART DIRECTION:** Raoul Giménez and Volker Spengler. **MAKEUP:** Anni Nöbauer. **SOUND:** Jean Luc Marié and Milan Bor. **MUSIC:** Peer Raben. **ASS'T DIRECTOR:** Juliane Lorenz. **PROD'N MANAGER:** Harry Baer.

With Volker Spengler (August Brem), Bulle Ogier (Hilde Krieger), Hanna Schygulla (Susanne Gast), Harry Baer (Rudolf Mann), Udo Kier (Edgar Gast), Margit Carstensen (Petra Vielhaber), Günther Kaufmann (Franz Walsch), Eddie Constantine (P. J. Lurz), Vitus Zeplichal (Bernhard von Stein), Raoul Giménez (Paul), Y Sa Lo (Ilse Hoffmann), Hark Bohm (Gerhard Gast), Lilo Pempeit (Mother Gast).
Shot in Berlin, December 1978–January 1979. Color, 35mm. 110 minutes.

Hanna Schygulla

"On *Maria Braun* RWF said to me, 'The costumes are more important than the sets for me because the sets don't change as quickly. I want to convey through the costumes what phase of the war and postwar periods we are in, and I would like to make clear through the costumes how the Economic Miracle unfolds, in general and in particular, through the career of Maria Braun.' He didn't have to say any more; with that the direction was clearly defined."

Barbara Baum, 1990

Elisabeth Trissenaar, Volker Spengler

"The film *In a Year of 13 Moons* is told through the encounters of a man during the last five days of his life and it tries, on the basis of these encounters, to figure out whether this man's decision, that on the final day, the fifth, he will allow no further days to follow, that he will refuse, is somehow understandable, or perhaps is even acceptable."

RWF, 1978

What does the title The Third Generation *refer to?*
"It refers to the three generations of terrorism, a theme that unfortunately is very fashionable. The first generation was that of '68. Idealists who wanted to change the world and told themselves they could do it with words and demonstrations. The second, the Baader-Meinhof group, went from legality to armed struggle and to total criminality. The third is that of today, which simply acts without thinking, which has neither ideology nor politics, and which, without knowing it, lets itself be controlled by others like a bunch of marionettes."

RWF, 1978

Margit Carstensen, Günther Kaufmann

1979/80

Berlin Alexanderplatz

Published in Germany in 1929, Alfred Döblin's *Berlin Alexanderplatz* is a classic of modern literature. After serving four years for beating to death the mistress he pimped, Franz Biberkopf, former day laborer, is released from Tegel prison and returns to Berlin determined to lead a decent life. The time is 1927, and in spite of Biberkopf's determination, as Döblin writes in his introduction, "something unaccountable crashes against him . . . with fraud and foul play. Three times Biberkopf is able to stand up again, but finally this thing torpedoes him with ferocious savagery," and he decides to end his life. But before Biberkopf can kill himself, a very unusual thing happens, and he is led to understand that his awful life had meaning, and he is given, so to speak, a radical cure. Biberkopf reappears in Berlin on Alexanderplatz, bruised but a new man.

Storyboard, with sketches by RWF

In thirteen parts and an epilogue. Part one: "Die Strafe beginnt" ("The Punishment Begins"); part two: "Wie soll man leben, wenn man nicht sterben will" ("How Is One to Live If One Doesn't Want to Die"); part three: "Ein Hammer auf den Kopf kann die Seele verletzen" ("A Hammer Blow on the Head Can Injure the Soul"); part four: "Eine Handvoll Menschen in der Tiefe der Stille" ("A Handful of People in the Depths of Silence"); part five: "Ein Schnitter mit der Gewalt vom lieben Gott" ("A Reaper with the Power of Our Lord"); part six: "Eine Liebe, das kostet immer viel" ("A Love Always Costs a Lot"); part seven: "Merke—einen Schwur kann man amputieren" ("Remember—An Oath Can Be Amputated"); part eight: "Die Sonne wärmt die Haut, die sich manchmal verbrennt" ("The Sun Warms the Skin, Which It Sometimes Burns"); part nine: "Von den Ewigkeiten zwischen den vielen und den wenigen" ("Of the Eternities Between the Many and the Few"); part ten: "Einsamkeit reisst auch in Mauern Risse des Irrsinns" ("Loneliness Makes Cracks of Madness in Walls, Too"); part eleven: "Wissen ist Macht, und Morgenstund hat Gold im Mund" ("Knowledge Is Power, and Early to Bed, Early to Rise"); part twelve: "Die Schlange in der Seele der Schlange" ("The Serpent in the Soul of the Serpent"); part thirteen: "Das Äussere und das Innere, und das Geheimnis der Angst vor der Angst" ("The External and the Internal, and the Secret of Fear of the Fear"); epilogue: "Rainer Werner Fassbinder—Mein Traum vom Traum des Franz Biberkopf" ("My Dream of Franz Biberkopf's Dream").

Bavaria Atelier/RAI television, in association with Westdeutscher Rundfunk. **PRODUCER:** Peter Märthesheimer. **SCREENPLAY:** Rainer Werner Fassbinder, from the novel by Alfred Döblin. **CAMERA:** Xaver Schwarzenberger. **ASS'T CAMERA:** Josef Vavra. **EDITING:** Juliane Lorenz and *Franz Walsch* (i.e., Rainer Werner Fassbinder). **SPECIAL EFFECTS:** Theo Nischwitz. **ART DIRECTION:** Helmut Gassner, Werner Achmann, and Jürgen Henze. **DECORATORS:** Hans Bussler and Tina Ruhl. **COSTUMES:** Barbara Baum. **MAKEUP:** Peter Knöpfle and Anni Nöbauer. **SOUND:** Karsten Ulrich and Milan Bor. **MUSIC:** Peer Raben. **ASS'T DIRECTORS:** Harry Baer and Renate Leiffer. **PROD'N MANAGER:** Dieter Minx.

With Günter Lamprecht (Franz Biberkopf), Hanna Schygulla (Eva), Barbara Sukowa (Mieze), Gottfried John (Reinhold), Franz Buchrieser (Meck), Claus Holm (Wirt), Brigitte Mira (Frau Bast), Roger Fritz (Herbert), Werner Asam (Fritz), Karin Baal (Mina), Harry Baer (Richard), Wolfgang Bathke (Redner), Alex Bayer (Dreske), Hark Bohm (Lüders), Liselotte Eder (Mrs. Pums), Irm Hermann (Trude), Günther Kaufmann (Theo), Vitus Zeplichal (Rudi), Margit Carstensen (Terah), Elisabeth Trissenaar (Lina), Barbara Valentin (Ida).
Shot in Berlin and Munich, June 1979–April 1980. Color, 16mm. Part one: 81 minutes; parts two–five: 59 minutes; parts six–nine: 58 minutes; parts ten–thirteen: 59 minutes; epilogue: 111 minutes.

Berlin Street Scene

Barbara Sukowa

"For Franz Biberkopf, it is not that he dies, but that what is anarchic in him dies. Of course he isn't a complete anarchist, since anarchy, insofar as I understand it, always has to have something to do with awareness. The anarchic in him is instead something childlike, unconscious, and it dies. And after that he is born again, and in a sense it's a rebirth, as a normal, middle-of-the-road guy who has little in common with the earlier Franz Biberkopf, who has in fact experienced extreme contradictions, for example just before the brawls with the communists, where he takes his first steps toward law and order, though he is a man who completely rejects law and order. But in place of that fellow there is now the epitome of the narrow-minded German bourgeois. And by that I also mean that in my opinion he ends up a Nazi."

RWF, 1980

Gottfried John, Barbara Sukowa

Günther Lamprecht, Hanna Schygulla, Roger Fritz

1980
Lili Marleen

In 1938 Zurich, Willie Bunterberg, a German national and cabaret singer, is having an affair with the club's pianist, Robert Mendelssohn, who would prefer to be a serious musician. Unbeknownst to Willie, Robert's wealthy father David is the head of an organization that spirits Jews out of Germany, and Robert is a principal operative. Fearful that his son's relationship with Willie will jeopardize his activities, David sees to it that Willie is not permitted to return to Switzerland after a visit to Germany. War breaks out and Willie becomes a recording star in Nazi Germany. The song she sings, "Lili Marleen," loved by millions of soldiers, is loathed by Goebbels as depressing but admired by Hitler. Willie is set up in luxury and is insulated from the truths of the Third Reich. Robert, missing her terribly, enters Germany in disguise.

Roxy-Film/Rialto-Film/CIP/Bayerischer Rundfunk. **PRODUCER:** Luggi Waldleitner, in association with Enzo Peri. **SCREENPLAY:** Rainer Werner Fassbinder after the unproduced screenplays of Joshua Sinclair and Manfred Purzer, from Lale Andersen's autobiography *Der Himmel hat viele Farben*. **CAMERA:** Xaver Schwarzenberger. **ASS'T CAMERA:** Josef Vavra. **EDITING:** Juliane Lorenz and *Franz Walsch* (i.e., Rainer Werner Fassbinder). **SPECIAL EFFECTS:** Joachim Schulz. **ART DIRECTION:** Rolf Zehetbauer. **COSTUMES:** Barbara Baum. **MAKEUP:** Anni Nöbauer. **SOUND:** Karsten Ulrich. **MUSIC:** Peer Raben. **CHOREOGRAPHY:** Dieter Gackstetter. **ASS'T DIRECTOR:** Renate Leiffer. **PROD'N MANAGER:** Konstantin Thoeren.

With Hanna Schygulla (Willie Bunterberg), Giancarlo Giannini (Robert Mendelssohn), Mel Ferrer (David Mendelssohn), Karl-Heinz von Hassel (Hans Henkel), Christine Kaufmann (Miriam Glaubrecht), Hark Bohm (Taschner), Karin Baal (Anna Lederer), Udo Kier (Drewitz), Gottfried John (Aaron), Lilo Pempeit (Tamara), Rainer Werner Fassbinder (Günther Weisenborn).
Shot in Berlin, and Munich and vicinity, July–September 1980, in English. Color, 35mm. 120 minutes.

1981
Lola

Set in a small city in the north of Bavaria in 1957, the film opens with a photograph of Konrad Adenauer, Chancellor of the Federal Republic of Germany since 1949. West Germany is in the midst of its Economic Miracle. Lola, the star performer at the cabaret (downstairs) and brothel (upstairs), where the city's politicians and businessmen gather, is the mistress of Schuckert, one of the city's principal developers, and mother of his child. Schuckert, married to an aristocratic woman aware of his relationship with Lola, complains to Lola about von Bohm, the newly arrived, middle-aged, idealistic building commissioner. Lola is amused that von Bohm intimidates the powerful Schuckert and arranges to meet the recent arrival. Unaware of Lola's various associations, von Bohm begins an affair with her. The film is dedicated to Alexander Kluge.

Rialto-Film/Trio-Film/Westdeutscher Rundfunk. **PRODUCER:** Horst Wendlandt. **SCREENPLAY:** Peter Märthesheimer, Pea Fröhlich, and Rainer Werner Fassbinder. **CAMERA:** Xaver Schwarzenberger. **ASS'T CAMERA:** Josef Vavra. **EDITING:** Juliane Lorenz. **LIGHTING:** Ekkehard Heinrich. **ART DIRECTION:** Raoul Giménez, Udo Kier, and Helmut Gassner. **COSTUMES:** Barbara Baum and Egon Strasser. **MAKEUP:** Anni Nöbauer and Gerd Nemetz. **SOUND:** Vladimir Vizner. **MUSIC:** Peer Raben. **ASS'T DIRECTOR:** Karin Viesel. **PROD'N MANAGER:** Thomas Schühly.

With Barbara Sukowa (Lola), Armin Mueller-Stahl (von Bohm), Mario Adorf (Schuckert), Matthias Fuchs (Esslin), Helga Feddersen (Hettich), Ivan Desny (Wittich), Karin Baal (Lola's mother), Rosel Zech (Mrs. Schuckert), Hark Bohm (Völker), Raoul Giménez and Udo Kier (waiters), Harry Baer (demonstrator).
Shot in Munich, April–May 1981. Color, 35mm. 113 minutes.

Hanna Schygulla

"In *Lili Marleen* I have a main character who is driven more by emotion than by thought. With that in mind I have tried to base the direction of the film on emotions. And for that I also need music. With music you can make a lot of people crazy because it's so suggestive. In general, when something happens in the story, there's music. It was not without good reason that Hitler suppressed such shows, sentimental ones, like in the Sports Palace. Music is also a way to keep people in line."

RWF, 1980

"*Maria Braun* and *Lola* are stories that are only possible in the time when the story takes place. And they are, as I hope, parts of a comprehensive portrait of the Federal Republic of Germany that make it easier for this peculiar democratic structure to be understood—also the threats and dangers. To that extent these are very political films. That I made *Lili Marleen* is more an accident. It is my first film about the Third Reich. And I would certainly make still more films about the Third Reich, but it is a separate theme, just as the Weimar Republic is a separate theme. I also want to pursue these thematic cycles. Perhaps there will be in the end a comprehensive picture of the German bourgeoisie since 1848. That would be my hope if I get far enough to make that many films. I find that everything has its logic. I also find that the Third Reich was not such an accident, it was not like history got injured on the job, the way it's often portrayed."

RWF, 1980

Barbara Sukowa

1981

Theater in Trance

A documentary in fourteen parts made during the 1981 World Theater Festival in Cologne. The soundtrack includes Fassbinder reading from Antonin Artaud's *The Theater and Its Double*.

Laura-Film, in association with Zweites Deutsches Fernsehen.
PRODUCER: Thomas Schühly. **SCREENPLAY:** Rainer Werner Fassbinder, with texts by Antonin Artaud. **CAMERA:** Werner Lüring. **EDITING:** Juliane Lorenz and *Franz Walsch* (i.e., Rainer Werner Fassbinder). **SOUND:** Vladimir Vizner. **ASS'T DIRECTOR:** Raoul Giménez and Karin Viesel.

With the dance and theater companies Het Werktheater, Amsterdam; Squat Theater, New York; Sombras Blancas, Mexico; Kipper Kids; Magazini Criminali, Florence; Pina Bausch and the Dance Theater Wuppertal; Jérôme Savary; Yoshi Oida. Shot in Cologne, June 1981. Color, 16mm. 91 minutes.

1982

Die Sehnsucht der Veronika Voss (Veronika Voss)

An actress popular during the Third Reich, and perhaps once the mistress of Goebbels, Veronika Voss lives in Munich ten years after the war. The city is experiencing an economic resurrection, but Voss is not. One rainy night walking through the park, she is offered help by Robert Krohn, a young sportswriter who does not recognize her. She later invites Robert to a restaurant, and he becomes fascinated by this strange but beguiling lady. They become lovers, and Robert discovers Voss is not only an addict but is being exploited by her doctor and the doctor's high-ranking accomplices.

Laura-Film/Tango-Film/Rialto-Film/Trio-Film/Maran-Film.
PRODUCER: Thomas Schühly. **SCREENPLAY:** Peter Märthesheimer, Pea Fröhlich, and Rainer Werner Fassbinder. **CAMERA:** Xaver Schwarzenberger. **ASS'T CAMERA:** Josef Vavra. **EDITING:** Juliane Lorenz. **ART DIRECTION:** Rolf Zehetbauer. **COSTUMES:** Barbara Baum. **MAKEUP:** Anni Nöbauer and Gerd Nemetz. **SOUND:** Vladimir Vizner. **MUSIC:** Peer Raben. **ASS'T DIRECTORS:** Karin Viesel, Harry Baer, and Tamara Kafka.

With Rosel Zech (Veronika Voss), Hilmar Thate (Robert Krohn), Cornelia Froboess (Henriette), Annemarie Düringer (Dr. Katz), Doris Schade (Josefa), Armin Mueller-Stahl (Max Rehbein), Günther Kaufmann (GI accomplice), Volker Spengler (first director), Juliane Lorenz (secretary), Rainer Werner Fassbinder (moviegoer). Shot in Munich, November–December 1981. B/W, 35mm. 104 minutes.

1982

Querelle

Set in the fabled port of Brest, *Querelle* charts the degradation and salvation of a beautiful sailor, Querelle, who murders a mate, allows himself to be sodomized as "execution" for the crime, and beds Madame Lysiane, the mistress of the brothel where sailors mingle with the underworld of Brest. Querelle and Gil, a fugitive murderer, enjoy a tender relationship until Querelle turns Gil over to Mario, the sadistic police inspector. Querelle returns to his ship, commanded by Lieutenant Sablon who, longing for Querelle, keeps his distance to tell the sailor's story. The film is dedicated "to my friendship with El Hedi ben Salem m'Barek Mohammed Mustafa—Rainer Werner Fassbinder."

Planet-Film/Albatros-Produktion/Gaumont, in association with Sam Waynberg.
PRODUCER: Dieter Schidor. **SCREENPLAY:** Rainer Werner Fassbinder, from Jean Genet's novel *Querelle de Brest*. **CAMERA:** Xaver Schwarzenberger. **EDITING:** Juliane Lorenz and *Franz Walsch* (i.e., Rainer Werner Fassbinder). **ART DIRECTION:** Rolf Zehetbauer. **COSTUMES:** Barbara Baum. **MAKEUP:** Ingrid Masmann-Korner and Gerd Nemetz. **SOUND:** Vladimir Vizner. **MUSIC:** Peer Raben. **ARTISTIC COLLABORATOR:** Harry Baer. **ASS'T DIRECTOR:** Karin Viesel.

With Brad Davis (Querelle), Franco Nero (Lieutenant Seblon), Jeanne Moreau (Lysiane), Laurent Malet (Roger), Hanno Pöschl (Robert/Gil), Günther Kaufmann (Nono), Burkhard Driest (Mario), Dieter Schidor (Vic), Harry Baer (Armenier). Shot in Berlin, March 1982. Color, 35mm. 106 minutes.

Rosel Zech

"I want with this film to give contemporary society something like a restoration
of history. Our democracy is one ordained
at a certain time for the Western Zone;
we didn't have to fight for it. Old patterns
have a good chance of finding a way
in—without the swastika, of course,
but through being educated in the old
ways. . . . I want to show how the 1950s
shaped the people of the sixties—this
collision of the establishment with the
activists that resulted in the abnormality
of terrorism."

RWF, 1982

"*Querelle de Brest* . . . is maybe the most radical novel in
world literature to deal with the discrepancy between
objective action and subjective fantasy. The superficial
plot, detached from Jean Genet's world of imagery, is an
uninteresting, rather third-class crime story. . . . What
makes it worthwhile, is the way the story unfolds through
Genet's way of telling it, with a remarkable fantasy that
at first conjures up an alien world that seems to have its
own rules, that is burdened with an astounding mythology.
But then it's really exciting and thrilling to discover . . .
how this strange world with its own laws relates to our
reality, which is also obviously experienced subjectively,
and draws astonishing truths from our reality because
it confronts us with recognitions and decisions, with the
result, and I am completely aware of the pathos, that
these specific recognitions may be so painful that they
bring us nearer to our own life."

RWF, 1982

Brad Davis

Curriculum Vitae

I was born on May 31, 1945, at Bad Wörishofen, the son of Dr. Helmuth Fassbinder, a general practitioner, and his wife, Liselotte, née Pempeit.

My early years were spent in Munich where, from 1951 to 1955, I attended the Rudolf Steiner School.

From 1955 to 1961, I attended the following high schools: 1955 to 1956, Theresiengymnasium, Munich; 1956 to 1958, St. Anna Gymnasium, Augsburg; 1958 to 1959, Realgymnasium, Augsburg; 1959 to 1961, Neues Realgymnasium, Munich.

From 1961 to 1963, I helped my father set up a real estate office in Cologne. During this time I also attended night school.

From 1963 to March 1964, I attended drama classes with the director Kraus in Munich. Subsequently, until May 31, 1966, I studied at the Fridl Leonhard Acting Studio.

From the end of July until early August 1966, I worked on Bruno Joris's television documentary *Hoffnungsgruppe* in Verona. After making my own 8mm films in September and October 1966, I completed my first short theatrical film in 35mm, *The City Tramp*, in November 1966. In addition, I won an award in November 1966 for *Just a Slice of Bread* in a drama contest of the Jungen Akademie of Munich. In February 1967, I made my second short 35mm film, *The Little Chaos*.

RWF, July 21, 1967

70	Ensemble
71	Warum läuft R. Amok
72	Nasty Kamera, ... , Harma
73	Händler der 4 Jahreszeiten
74	Die bitteren Tränen Margot Carstensen, Eva Mattes,
75	Angst essen Seele auf B. Mira
76	Wildwechsel
77	
78	Despair
79	Maria Braun

FASSBINDER
BERLIN ALEXANDERPLATZ
14
MEINTRAUM
VOM DELIRIUM
des Franz Biberkopf
VON
ALFRED DÖBLIN

$$258$$

73
17
72
43
47
5
96
2
47
82
29
3081
83
665

$$4455 : 60 = 74$$
$$255$$

$$2250$$

24	Lili Marleen kelte als der Tod	80
34	Kekelmacher	80
5	Götter der Pest	85
36	Warum läuft Herr R. Amok	85
22	Rio das Mortes	80
21	Whity	85
11	Niklashauser Fart	90
23	Jakob der Soldat	
2	Warnung vor einer heiligen Nutte	120
28	Pioniere in Ingolstadt	105
16	Händler der vier Jahreszeiten	85
20	Die bitteren Tränen der Petra von Kant	90
25	Acht Stunden	100
19	Acht Stunden	85
32	Acht Stunden 2	80
27	Acht Stunden	105
17	Acht Stunden	95
		95
6	Effi Briest	125
12	Angst essen Seele auf	90
15	Welt am Draht	210
10	Faustrecht der Freiheit	105
7	Martha	115
18	Mutter Küsters	95
26	Angst vor der Angst	90
9	Satansbraten	120
31	Ich will doch nur, dass ihr mich liebt	90
18	Chinesisches Roulette	80
30	Bolwieser	185
1	Respekt	125
13	Deutschland im Herbst	20
29	Frauen in New York	125
8	Die Ehe der Maria Braun	120
3	Ihr Jahr ist spenden	95
14	Die 3. Generation	90
4	Berlin Alexanderplatz	

$$4455$$

75 Stunden 30 Min

Notes by RWF
assessing his films.
1980

Reflections of a Vertex

I am the vertex of a triangle. The two lines converging in me form an obtuse angle that should offer me a view into the future. But my future is very uncertain. Even a little schoolboy with an eraser can plunge my future into total nothingness. Every day I expect such a mortal blow, hoping all the while that I may be spared. At times I believe that for us who are vertices there should be a midpoint, toward which we draw nearer every day, in order to meld with it or lose ourselves in it. But when days go by without the slightest change in my situation, I come close to despair. Though I might maintain that each day I gain greater insight into the cruelties of the world, they don't even spare an innocent vertex. I often tell myself that one of my two lines must be put down incorrectly or be wrong. I am thinking less of the baseline, which exists beyond any doubt; no, I'm thinking of side B, which I can't quite get a view of, since in contrast to the baseline, it appears to be crooked or wrongly placed. I sincerely wish I could change line B, guide it into an orderly path. But I keep failing because of the many interruptions this line is prone to. A point simply can't reach across an empty space. I often wonder what would have happened if lines B and C had bypassed each other, had never touched, let alone converged. True, at present their paths are wide apart. But I, the vertex, remain, and unfortunately I am the spot where the two lines meet, though line A remotely connects them at a distance. I often think it might be best for me to quietly sneak away from my existence as a vertex. But so far I haven't found the right way to make myself do it. Perhaps I am too much of a coward or too scared of eternity, which, I am sure, no God could sweeten for me. I confess I haven't yet come to an all-consuming end. But I keep working on it, and perhaps I'll find a way for the lines and myself to be reconciled.

RWF, 1959

The Application
Hans Helmut Prinzler

On September 17, 1966, the Deutsche Film-und Fernsehakademie Berlin (German Film and Television Academy, Berlin) opened. At this time, thirty-two male and three female students began their studies. Rainer Werner Fassbinder was not among them: he had failed the entrance exam. Years later, when Fassbinder had become better known than any of the graduates of the first academic year, the failure was blamed on the examiners. The commission, not the candidate, had failed. It had obviously overlooked a genius. But doesn't every commission, deciding on ability and talent, run the risk of making poor judgments?

Since we have no way of comparing it with the work of the other applicants, there is not much point in examining the work Fassbinder submitted for the entrance examination in Berlin to determine whether his rejection was justified. Yet the exam papers make fascinating reading as to how Rainer Werner Fassbinder argued and wrote in the spring of 1966. He was twenty years old at the time.

"Dear Sirs," Rainer Werner Fassbinder wrote on February 3, 1966, to the Secretary's Office of the DFFB. "If there is still time to apply for entrance examinations at your academy, I would appreciate your informing me of the conditions for admission. Yours sincerely, . . ."

At the time, 825 applicants had requested application forms. Most of them must have found the questionnaire intimidating, for by the deadline of March 31, 1966, only 245 applications had arrived in Berlin. Documents required for participation in the entrance exams were: a graduation certificate from high school at least, subsequent employment or university studies, and age between twenty-three and twenty-eight (though exceptions were taken into consideration).

Application forms had to be accompanied by: recommendations, proofs of employment, samples of the applicant's artistic work such as films, photographs, drawings, poems, short stories, plays, screenplays, etc.

Fassbinder sent neither recommendations nor proof of employment. Instead he wrote: "I am an actor but I only just had the opportunity of taking final exams at the Theater Association. The date is April 18, 1966. As of now, I have not been employed in the theater." As a sample of his artistic work he submitted "Parallels: Notes and Text for a Film."

The examining commission, consisting of the two DFFB directors, Erwin Leiser and Heinz Rathsack, and two professors, Ulrich Gregor and Peter Lilienthal, invited seventy-four applicants to the entrance exams in Berlin. About Fassbinder, Lilienthal noted: "Actor, twenty years old, submitted a treatment of a screenplay, remarkable for his age." Leiser: "'Parallels' shows promise and is striking in its impact. Should be admitted to entrance exams."

The entrance exams were held from May 23 to 26, 1966, in Berlin. There were both written and practical exams. Practical meant: an exercise with an 8mm camera. Twenty applicants who had work experience were excused from the practical exams. Students were given film; the film was to run less than 8 minutes and had to be comprehensible without sound. Fassbinder shot a film which unfortunately has not survived.

The first part of the written exam consisted of twenty-six questions. Excerpts from this part follow.

Question 1: A famous 19th-century novel concerns the war between Russia and France, then ruled by Napoleon. **a)** What is the name of the novel? **b)** Who is the author? **c)** Have you read the novel? If so, did you like it? **d)** Has this novel been made into a film? (When, by whom?)
Fassbinder: a) *War and Peace.* **b)** Leo Tolstoy. **c)** No. **d)** In 1956, by King Vidor (USA); in 1965, in the USSR.

Question 2: Name a director in the 1930s whose work you are interested in. Tell something about a film of his that made the greatest impression on you.
Fassbinder: Jean Vigo. Four years ago I had a chance to see *Zéro de conduite*. The film left a deep impression on me, though I don't remember the details. I know only that *Zéro de conduite* awakened in me the desire to make my own movies one day.

Question 3: What is "Commedia dell'Arte"?
Fassbinder: "Commedia dell'Arte" is the art of making even the smallest movements in the theater composed and well-balanced.

Question 4: What is the meaning of the word "ellipse" in the context of screenwriting? Can you give an example?
Fassbinder: (not answered)

Question 5: Former Chancellor Adenauer recently visited Israel. How do you view the present German–Israeli relationship after that trip?
Fassbinder: (not answered)

Question 6: a) What novel have you read lately? How do you rate it? **b)** Which nonfiction or science book have you read lately? How do you rate it?
Fassbinder: John Rechy, *City of Night*. In my opinion, *City of Night* is a novel in which the best of realism (especially in the dialogues) alternates with inane chatter (in the main character's self-analysis).

Question 7: Which artistic means of expression are shared by novel and film? Which means of expression exist only in film, which only in the novel?
Fassbinder: Language. Not being bound by space or time. The moving picture. The use of music in film, the inner monologue; the use of language as a narrative element in the novel.

Question 8: If you were to make a movie of a stage play of your choice, which play would you choose? What is your interest in this material?
Fassbinder: *Lunch Break*, by John Mortimer. *Lunch Break* has a small, simple story around which and from which a film with a socially critical emphasis could be made.

Question 9: Have you seen or read anything by Beckett?

Fassbinder: Yes (*Murphy*, *Molloy*, *Krapp's Last Tape*, *The Way It Is*, *Endgame*, *Coming and Going*.)

Question 10: What made Darwin famous?
Fassbinder: His theory of the steady evolution from the most primitive beings to man.

Question 11: What, in your opinion, has Brecht to offer a person who wants to make a movie?
Fassbinder: The alienation effect, which in movies can be applied in a variety of ways.

Question 12: When did the last Party Congress of the Communist Party of the Soviet Union take place? Can you relate some of the most important events of this Party Congress? How did this Party Congress affect world politics?
Fassbinder: a) In 1966. **b)** Steps were taken to rehabilitate Stalin. The USSR made efforts to form a new friendship with the Chinese bloc in the context of Communist ideology. **c)** The Congress established ideological guidelines on Communist policy for the Soviet bloc.

Question 13: Name a work by Beckett with which you are familiar and briefly evaluate it.
Fassbinder: *Krapp's Last Tape*. A man tries to take stock of his life with the help of a tape recorder. The lack of meaning it reveals plunges him into total silence (which may last forever). In my opinion, *Krapp's Last Tape* is Beckett's best play. In it he is at his best showing the absurdity and ultimate senselessness of a human life.

Question 14: Is there any author, painter, stage director, or composer you admire? **a)** Which one? **b)** Why?
Fassbinder: Yes. **a)** Marcel Proust. **b)** Because *Remembrance of Things Past* is the most lucid and sensitive self-analysis I know.

Question 15: a) When did you last see a movie? **b)** Which one? **c)** Who was the author of the screenplay, the director, the cinematographer, the producer, and who were the main actors? **d)** Briefly describe the contents. **e)** Give a brief review of the film.
Fassbinder: a) On May 20, 1966. **b)** *A Married Woman*. **c)** Jean-Luc Godard/Jean-Luc Godard/Raoul Coutard/Macha Meril/Phillipe Leroy/Bernard Noel. **d)** A woman and her lover are in bed together, talking about themselves. He wants her to leave her husband and marry him.

They must go, and they get dressed. The man, an actor, drives the woman into town in his car. Since the husband once had her followed, they take detours, and the woman continues alone, changing taxis several times. She picks up her husband's son from kindergarten, drives with him to the airport, where her husband, an aviator, has just arrived with a friend. They invite the friend for dinner, in the course of which a conversation develops about their respective views on life. There follows another sequence in bed, this time with the woman and her husband. Next day, the actor unexpectedly departs by plane to perform in a provincial theater. He arranges to meet the woman in the airport cinema. After a talk with her maid and a visit to a spa, she meets her lover in the cinema, which is showing Resnais's *Night and Fog*. They leave the cinema during the performance. The movie's third bed sequence, during which the woman questions the actor, among other things, about his profession, follows. She decides to return to her husband. **e)** Godard calls *A Married Woman* "fragments of a picture." The bed sequences consist of single closeups of various parts of the body; the rest of the story is continuously interrupted by photos of ads, supposedly reflecting the heroine's emotional frame of mind. Here lies the weakness of "fragments of a picture." I don't believe it is possible to reveal a character by letting her leaf through fashion magazines, suggesting that she wants to be shaped by contemporary advertising; least of all a character like Macha Meril, with her impressive and highly individualistic face, who, during the conversation about attitudes toward life in the middle of the film, opts for the present and whose arguments seem to me the most intelligent of the three. *A Married Woman* is a beautiful film, clear in its details but, to my mind, not sufficiently thought through. This impression may have been created by the movie's truly fragmented character; the overall concept is certainly revealed in what has been left out.

Question 16: Could you briefly describe the difference between the constitutional position of the President of the Federal Republic of Germany and that of the former President of the German Reich?
Fassbinder: No.

*Bolwieser (The
Stationmaster's Wife).*
1977/83. Armin Meier,
Volker Spengler

Question 17: Do you know a movie in which an amateur actor plays the leading role? How do you rate this performance? In general, how do you feel about entrusting amateurs with leading roles?

Fassbinder: *Il Posto [The Postal Worker]* by Ermanno Olmi. I thought the actor who played Il Posto was outstanding, and I'm inclined to regard his performance as one of the best theatrical works in pictures. You could see all the tragedy of a life that had been worthless from the start in his eyes. Perhaps in his case it was less a question of acting skills than of being able to remain completely himself. In some cases working with untrained actors certainly has its advantages. But on the whole I prefer "trained actors." In most cases, an untrained actor is likely to lose his unselfconsciousness before the camera and with that he loses the expression he was chosen for. Then it is up to

him to retrieve that expression. The search for the right expression is the actor's job, which is difficult and, in general, can be achieved only through training.

Question 18: Aside from film, is there an artistic medium you would like to use? If so, which one and why?

Fassbinder: Writing, because I am fascinated by the use of language in whatever shape or form.

Question 19: What function can color take on in film?

Fassbinder: It is conceivable that by using color, one can highlight the emotional condition of the film's characters. I know only one example where one might say this has been achieved: Antonioni's *Red Desert*.

Question 22: What poetry have you read lately?
Fassbinder: Walt Whitman, *Leaves of Grass*.

Question 25: Name a film in which sound has a prominent artistic effect, and explain why.
Fassbinder: In M. Antonioni's film *Red Desert*, the almost relentless sound of engines is supposed to highlight the loneliness of the main character. Also the use of electronic music, in this case almost equivalent to a sound screen, is apparently meant to describe the nature of the heroine's illness.

Question 26: What do you know about Eisenstein?
Fassbinder: Eisenstein was one of the greatest film theoreticians. The use of montage, music, color, and actors in film was theoretically articulated and developed by him.

The second part of the written test was the filmic adaptation of a short story. The commission chose the story "The Little-Girls-Eater" by Septimus Dale. In a treatment of between three and five pages, the applicants were asked to explore how this story could be made into a movie. In addition, they had to prepare an outline of twenty-five scenes.

The Little-Girls-Eater
Treatment by Rainer Werner Fassbinder

A mother stands on a street with her daughter, waiting for her lover. The mother is about forty years old, but the way she is dressed for the date makes her appear somewhat younger. She wears too much makeup. Her dress, a little scanty for her plump body, makes her seem heavy. Her daughter's name is Miranda. She looks like Catherine Demongeot in *Zazie*. But, unlike *Zazie*, she wears a girlish, light, summer dress.

The little girl is trying to speak to her mother. But the mother, fixed on the imminent event, seems absent-minded and barely reacts to the child's questions. To attract her mother's attention, Miranda remarks that a dead dog is lying in the street. Infuriated by her daughter's fib, the mother scolds her, which makes Miranda burst into tears.

At that moment Johnny, the mother's boyfriend, arrives in a beautiful car, which Miranda likes. Johnny is younger than Miranda's mother. Athletically built, he is dressed like an Italian gangster in an American movie. Johnny steps

out of the car, walks toward the mother, and embraces her. Miranda skips around the car, but when the embrace takes too long, she tugs at Johnny's sleeve and asks him where he got the car. Again the mother reprimands her, saying that children don't need to know everything.

Uncle Johnny is going to show Miranda the ocean. They get into the car and Johnny takes off. Sitting in the back, Miranda watches Uncle Johnny fondle, then pinch her mother's thigh. The mother enjoys this, but admonishes Johnny not to do it in front of the child.

For a while, Miranda keeps quiet. Then she observes that her Daddy never takes her to the beach and that she likes Uncle Johnny better than her father anyhow. The two in front take no notice. Johnny switches on the radio and with his other hand continues to fondle Miranda's mother.

Miranda stares at the ocean, which is gray, its beaches strewn with garbage, while Uncle Johnny draws her attention to the beautiful blue sea and goes on about its vastness.

At the end of a narrow lane, Johnny stops the car and all three get out. To make love (as they call it) in private, they send Miranda down to the beach.

Getting close to the water, Miranda spots an old coal dock whose intricate structure intrigues her. But the place looks scary and Miranda hesitates before she decides to go farther.

Not until she almost steps on him does Miranda notice a man with only his head and arms sticking out of the sand. A large log lies where his back begins. Hiding behind a concrete pillar, she watches the man, who is trying to reach a beat-up tin can with his hands. He actually grabs it and tries to scratch himself with the can, but being in the position he is in, he fails. In the end, he lowers his head onto the sand and utters a noise that sounds like a sob. When that, too, becomes silent, Miranda starts singing a song. It is the song of the bottles, standing on the wall, falling over one by one.

As Miranda comes to the third verse, the man joins in. Miranda runs over to him. He stops in the middle of the verse, raises his arms toward Miranda and utters a sound as though to frighten her. Miranda runs away.

Miranda's mother and Johnny stand by the car. He is closing the zipper on her mother's dress. Miranda runs up to them and tells them about the man she has seen by the dock. Her mother does not believe her and tells her to shut up. But when Miranda doesn't stop talking about the man with only his head and arms reaching up from the sand, Johnny takes over. He tells Miranda that it must be the little-girls-eater, who only comes out to kill little girls. Miranda falls silent, climbs into the car with her mother and Johnny, and they drive away.

EXCERPTS FROM FASSBINDER'S OUTLINE:

1. A brief view of the ocean and the beach from a side window of a large American car.

2. From the outside, the girl Miranda is seen through the windshield, staring wide-eyed into the distance.

3. A drive along the seashore. The water is grayish-green. Garbage is scattered along the beach. After a while:
Johnny, off-screen: Look, Miranda. The ocean. Blue and vast and beautiful. You see that?
Miranda, off-screen: Yes.
Johnny, off-screen: And the water never ends. It's endless. You understand that?
Miranda, off-screen: Yes.
Johnny, off-screen: It's quite simple. Here is America and somewhere over there, so far away you can't even imagine, there is Africa. There are more black people there even than over here.
Somewhat later:
Miranda, off-screen: I don't like the ocean.

4. Johnny in profile. He shrugs.
Johnny: Tough luck. The kid has a mind of her own.
The mother, off-screen: Too bad.

5. Miranda, closeup, looks wistfully into the camera.
Miranda: Why?

The main change Fassbinder made to the literary original is the perspective of the narrator. In Septimus Dale, Mason, the mysterious character on the beach, is the center of the story. A falling beam has plunged him into the dangerous position from which he cannot

free himself. As soon as the tide comes in, he will perish. Miranda, who is Fassbinder's central figure, is of only minor interest in Dale's story. Having come to the ocean with her mother and Johnny, she could become Mason's salvation. The story's element of suspense is whether the man will be freed from his fatal situation. Fassbinder turns the story into the psychogram of a lonely girl. To achieve that, he even foregoes the story's climax. After Johnny's fearful admonition, the three drive home. The man on the beach is left to himself. In Septimus Dale, Miranda returns to the injured man and, believing him to be the little-girls-eater, kills him with a stone.

Film criticism was the third part of the exam. Applicants were to present this in the form of a review in a daily paper, an essay in a professional magazine, or as an analysis. It was stressed that the applicants justify their opinions. There was a choice of three movies: *Vivre sa vie* (Godard), the short film *Incident at Owl Creek Bridge* (Robert Enrico), and the television documentary *Beat in Upper Bavaria*. Fassbinder wrote about *Vivre sa vie*:

The story of a consciousness: *Vivre sa vie*
    To this day, *Vivre sa vie*, Jean-Luc Godard's fourth full-length feature film, has remained the author's best. It is a didactic piece [*Lehrstück*], in the Brechtian sense, a film about a "modern" young woman, a documentary about prostitution, and a study of bistros and street life in Paris.
    The actual *Story of Nana S.*, as the film is called in Germany, is quickly told. Nana leaves her husband, whose child she has borne, "because things didn't work out," even though they liked each other, because she wants her freedom back. It becomes quite clear, though, that she has no talent for day-to-day living. When her money troubles become more and more pressing, she turns to prostitution. Yet she remains basically innocent until her death, which is horrible and senseless, at the end of the movie.
    Godard prefaces his film with a quotation from Montaigne: "One must surrender to others

and remain true to oneself." With this quotation in mind, he sets out to show the stages by which a person turns into a conscious human being.

He divides the story into twelve chapters, interrupting the flow of the action with chapter headings, thus never letting the viewer identify with the character and forcing him to follow his train of thought.

Each stage is clearly defined — at the start, for instance, the story of the chicken, which consists of an outside and an inside. If you take away the outside, the inside remains, and if you take that, too, the soul remains. Moreover, the stages are marked by the musical theme which is heard at regular intervals.

Other stages are Nana experiencing the suffering of *Jeanne d'Arc*, by Th. Dreyer; her statement after a police interrogation: "I want to become another person"; the first man she gives herself to (in a horrendous scene); her acquaintance with Paris prostitution; her encounter with a young man whom she will love; her realization of the interchangeability of her character; a conversation about love and language with the philosopher Brice Parani.

Vivre sa vie is a movie about love and language. Nana and the young man love one another. Godard expresses it like this: The young man reads to Nana a section from "The Oval Portrait," by Edgar Allan Poe, which is also indicative of Godard's very personal love for the actress who portrays Nana.

Anna Karina plays the part and is a marvel of genuine expression, believability, and life. The film's greatness and power to convince us are largely due to her.

Fassbinder in an interview: "There is one movie by Godard which I have seen twenty-seven times. That is *Vivre sa vie*. Together with *Viridiana* (by Buñuel), it has been the most important film in my life."

Today, a film review (there is a choice of two) is still part of the DFFB entrance exam.

The next test was an analysis of a sequence in a feature film. The applicants were presented with the first sequence of *Un Condamné à mort s'est échappé* by Robert Bresson. The title was not revealed. The test required careful observation of detail, recognition of style, description as to how it was achieved, and an overall evaluation.

FASSBINDER'S ANALYSIS:

The filmed sequence shows a prisoner's unsuccessful escape from a prison van, from the first attempt to the last consequence. The sequence consists of about forty setups, each one clear and simple, with no regard for superficial beauty.

Each setup makes sense only in connection with the preceding one and the one that succeeds it.

The necessary prerogatives for the escape — the fugitive, his hand, the door handle inside the car, a vehicle and a streetcar which force, or almost force, the prison van to stop — are clearly shown in their interrelationships. In relatively quick succession, we see first the fugitive, who stares ahead; then the road, where in a moment a vehicle may force the prison van to stop; then the fugitive's hand, reaching for the door handle.

Up to the moment of the escape, the setups change fairly rapidly; later they markedly slow down, as the main character is forced from activity into passivity. He has had little time for his flight, the police have ample time for his punishment.

The immense power of the police and the actual importance of the escape is less evident in the last setups with the battered fugitive than during the flight, where the other two prisoners don't even turn their heads when the shots ring out behind them.

With great sensitivity, the director refrains from showing the brutality visited on the escapee, who is carried, covered up on a stretcher. It is left to the viewer to use his imagination to picture the beaten-up man, so that later, when he sees the distorted, bloody face, he is not totally overcome by horror but is able to reflect on his attitude to such treatment.

The sequence has been thought through down to the smallest detail. It has been stripped of everything superfluous. The director sticks to the essentials.

Finally, the applicants were given an opportunity to submit an additional text of their choice. Choosing a letter, Fassbinder wrote:

Berlin, 24.5.66

Dear Mr. L.,
As a producer you probably have very little time. I therefore would like to thank you once again for granting me a relatively long and friendly conversation.

I am honored to think that we both enjoy Chagall. That is why I carefully chose the picture which at this moment most inspires me to turn it into a movie. It is *The Girl on the Horse*.

Here, as briefly as possible, is the plot. It is a Romeo-and-Juliet story, also somewhat reminiscent of *Käthchen von Heilbronn*, which I like very much.

Alexis and Jeanne met at a country dance and instantly knew that they belonged to each other. But their families are feuding and Jeanne's father locks up his daughter.

The young man will not give up hope, though. Day after day he hangs around by her house and finally even sleeps there.

The father loses patience and comes up with a cruel suggestion. They will be allowed to see and love each other in the marketplace. The boy is to play the fiddle, the girl is to sit on a horse. Love will last as long as does their strength.

If it doesn't, the girl will be sent to a convent, the boy will have to forget her. The scene in the marketplace takes place, but the townspeople, who earlier were prepared to laugh at the two, have realized that something sinister is happening and have stayed away.

The two are alone in the marketplace. She sits on the horse, which is standing still; he plays the fiddle.

So much for the story. It will not be easy to turn it into a movie, but if you could grant me a few small wishes, I believe I could make a beautiful picture.

First of all, the actors. If at all possible, I should like to have Anna Karina play the girl. The young man should be played by an actor who is not yet known but whose art I greatly respect and whom I would like to have with me while I work. He is going to be available.

The location I have chosen is Bad Wimpfen, a small town near Heilbronn in Baden. You may not know it, but Bad Wimpfen is a town where my story could actually happen or might have happened.

I'd like to see a movie every day, even while I am shooting. Also, I'd appreciate a small advance toward expenses. I quite often go hungry.

I can't think of any further requests. I am sure that under these circumstances I should be able to deliver a good product.

With hopeful regards,
Yours, R. Fassbinder

Not even his heartrending letter moved the commission. No notes have survived as to how other work Fassbinder submitted for the entrance exams was evaluated.

In 1967 Fassbinder applied again to the DFFB. He submitted two films (*The City Tramp* and *The Little Chaos*), the script for a television play, *Table Tennis*, and, in collaboration with applicant Susanna Schimkus, a script for a television play, *The Thirtieth Year*. The preselection committee rated him and his work as: "not sufficiently trained. Films: unsatisfactory." "Television play: good in dialogue, unpretentious." "Second application. Have read *Table Tennis*. Very conscientious, but unfortunately not substantial. Perhaps he should be tried, though, provided his own films give hope." "Films still unsatisfactory." Fassbinder was not invited to sit for the exams.

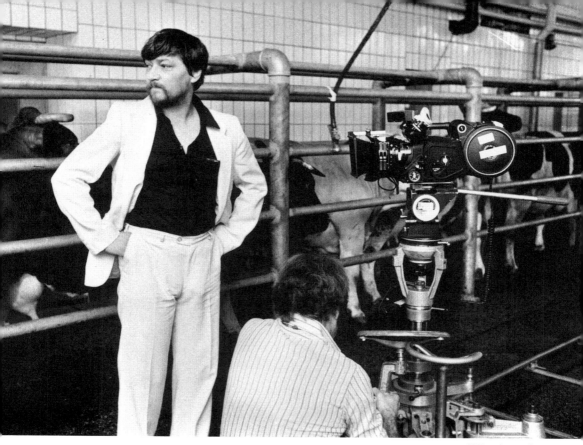

RWF on the set of
*In einem Jahr mit 13
Monden (In a Year of
13 Moons)*, 1978

Conversations with Rainer Werner Fassbinder
Christian Braad Thomsen

BERLIN, 1971

*Before you went into moviemaking, you wrote and produced for
the theater—or the antiteater, as you called it. Why did you actually start making films?*

I first made two short films. I went into the theater only after that. What
I did was not "anti-theater" but theater. *Antiteater* was just a name, like
a theater being named Schiller Theater. I learned a lot in the theater—
how to deal with actors and different ways to tell a story. I am also an
actor, by the way. Acting is the one thing I actually studied—in everything else I am self-taught.

Actually, I wanted to make movies right from the start, but it
wasn't easy. So I did what came easy, which is theater. This paid off,
because when I started making films, I found it easier, having come
from the theater. My success and the reason why my films were

accepted in the festivals had something to do with the fact that in Germany theater is more prestigious than film. People thought: "Sure, this guy has made films, but he has also done theater—there must be something there."

Many of your films have been influenced by early American gangster movies and melodramas, though they greatly differ from them. What do you like in the movies of Raoul Walsh and Douglas Sirk?

That isn't easy to explain. The stories these movies tell are quite simple and straightforward, yet full of suspense. Before I made *Whity*, I watched a number of films by Raoul Walsh, mainly *Band of Angels*, one of the most exciting movies I know, with Clark Gable, Yvonne de Carlo, and Sidney Poitier. A white farmer dies. He has a daughter by a black woman. The daughter is white, so it isn't evident that she is of mixed blood. But when the old man dies, deeply in debt, she is sold. Clark Gable plays the slave-trader who buys her. He knows she is half black, and she knows he is a slave-trader. Comes the Civil War. Sidney Poitier is the slave-trader's loyal servant and, although he fights on the opposite side, he helps his master escape with the girl, and everything turns out all right—or does it? Good directors manage to provide happy endings that still leave the viewers dissatisfied with the outcome of the movie. They know something isn't quite right. Things just don't work that way.

There are a few American movies I saw when I was young and still remember. I don't recall the titles, just the mood. American movies are the only ones I take seriously, because they reach their audience. Before 1933, German films did that too, and of course there are a few directors in other countries who are in touch with their audiences. But of American films one can say in general that they have a good relationship with their public. It's because they are not trying to be art. The way they tell a story is not complicated or artificial—of course it is artificial, but it's not arty. I don't like art.

But isn't the difference between Hollywood movies and your films precisely that your films are art?

True, but the difference is that a European director is not as naive as a Hollywood director. We always feel a need to reflect on what we are doing, why we are doing it, and how we will do it, though I am sure the day will come when I, too, shall be able to tell a perfectly naive story. I am trying to do that more and more, but it isn't easy. American directors operate on what seems a fairly wholesome level. Their political attitude is conservative, and they pretend that the U.S.A. is the land of freedom and justice. With that attitude they make their movies without scruples, which I find disarming. Yet, unlike the Italians, I have never tried to copy Hollywood movies, preferring to make movies based on our understanding of film—at least in the beginning.

When you say you only take films seriously that have an audience, do you mean you don't take your own films seriously? Let's face it, they hardly have an audience.

That has nothing to do with me but with the specific economic situation Germany is now caught up in. My films will find their audience once that situation changes. Right now German movie houses offer third-rate fare. Film has become a business and third-rate fare sells better than high quality. I am sure that will change. It has already changed in France; today Chabrol makes movies for large audiences. When he first started, he too made films for just a few. It took him twelve years to find his public.

Contrary to many so-called established directors, you appeal to the emotions in your films, which should suit the public's taste.

To me emotions are very important, but in our day emotions are being exploited by the movie industry, and this I abhor. I object to leaving emotions open to speculation and to having to pay for them.

This ambivalent attitude toward emotions you also express in your movies. You present a scene with a strong emotional impact, then you slow down the camera, creating a sort of abstraction.

Yes, it is a sort of abstraction. When you slow down a scene in progress, you can see what really happens in a story. You see what is going on and experience it with your emotions. If such a scene is edited, you no longer know what it was about.

So you consider these drawn-out scenes a sort of take-off on American genre films?

Not at all. Some critics believe that I was making ironic references to American genre films, which I can well understand. It may be interpreted that way and I must accept that interpretation, though for me it isn't like that at all. The difference between the American way of moviemaking and my own lies in the fact that American movies don't reflect. But then I myself would like to find a way of moviemaking that develops freely without such reflections. By the way, only half of my pictures bear any relation to American genre films. On the whole, I divide my films into two groups. There are the bourgeois films which play in narrowly defined middle-class settings, and the cinematographic films which play in typically cinematographic settings with a story we recognize from the world of cinema. The first group deals with specifically middle-class mechanisms; the other is inspired by various genres of film.

But don't genre films also play in middle-class settings?

Yes, the gangster setting is middle-class, only in reverse, with middle-class rather than alternative ideals. My gangsters are not rebels but victims of middle-class attitudes. If they were rebels, they would act differently. Their attitude is basically the same as that of capitalist and middle-class society, except the gangster's attitude is unlawful. In my films there is no basic difference between a gangster and a sleazy capitalist. A gangster has the same bourgeois desires as the ordinary citizen. Maybe here lies the difference between my films and American gangster movies. There the gangsters sometimes are true outsiders, whereas my small-time gangsters and thieves are basically integrated into society.

It very rarely happens that your characters actually rebel against the conditions they live in. Though it does happen in Whity, *where the slave kills his master and escapes.*

Yet in actual fact, the entire film is pitted against the black man, because he always hesitates and fails to defend himself against injustice. In the end he does shoot the people who oppressed him, but then he goes off into the desert and dies, having come to realize certain things without being able to act. He goes into the desert because he doesn't dare face the inevitable consequences. I find it OK that he kills his oppressors, but it is not OK that he then goes into the desert. For by doing that he accepts the superiority of the others. Had he truly believed in his action, he would have allied himself with other suppressed individuals, and they would have acted together. The singlehanded act at the end of the movie is not a solution. Thus, in the last instance the film turns even against blacks.

You provocatively stated that Whity *is not a movie about racism.*

When I made *Whity,* I never thought I was going to make a movie about racism, and when I made *Katzelmacher* I didn't say: "Now I'm going to make a film about foreign workers." Though that, people later claimed, was what *Katzelmacher* was about and what they gave me awards for. Nor did I mean to make a picture about Vietnam when I made *The American Soldier.* To me it was always important to make movies about people and their relationships, their dependence on each other and on society. My films are about dependence, a social work project, because dependence makes people unhappy, and conscious work on such a project means social work.

Do you feel an affinity to Brecht?

No, rather to the Austrian writer Odon von Horvath, who, unlike Brecht, is deeply interested in people. I might compare someone like Alexander Kluge to Brecht and compare myself to Horvath. Kluge's abstraction, like Brecht's, is intellectual, whereas mine is stylistic. Horvath and Brecht don't differ all that much in their political views, but rather in how they express them.

VENICE, 1971

How autobiographical is your new movie, Beware of a Holy Whore? Is it about the filming of a movie?

In some way or other, everything in this film is autobiographical, which doesn't mean that things happened the way they did in the movie.

How about the director's dictatorial working methods?

That does exist. There are moments when I am extremely dictatorial. I have made movies in other ways, but when I come under extreme pressure I turn into a dictator. When directing is difficult or when things go badly, there is a risk that people you work with may turn against you rather than support you. In that case, you have to resort to dictatorship.

You demonstrate that by having the director [in Beware] complete his film and grow in the process, yet his tyrannical attitude does not change. Is that correct? He completes his film, yet he does not change?

My director's positive development lies in the fact that he realizes the team is not a team and in abandoning the dream of the collective. He gives up his illusion and faces the situation as it is. I believe movies can be made in a less dictatorial way. But then you must say from the start: "I am the director, you are the cameraman, and you are the actors." If everyone's work is clearly defined, each person can focus on his part rather than have people share in everything, in which case nothing will be done right. It may sound dictatorial, but the moment this became clear to me, I acted much less like a dictator. There was this dream of our team, i.e., the team in the movie as well as the actual team, sharing responsibility and problems, letting everyone have a say in determining what movies should be and how and why they should be made. Unfortunately, it didn't work. I don't mean that it is impossible, and I still hope that in some way it can be done. But it didn't work in our case. People soon realized that if they did nothing, I would have to do all the more, in order to get the project finished at all. They increasingly relied on that. During the filming of *Whity* everything broke down. Suddenly people realized we had not accomplished what we had set out to do. *Beware of a Holy Whore* is basically about the filming of *Whity*.

To what extent are you working as a collective? For instance, are you living together, and do you also live together outside working hours?

We did share a house, but while we were shooting most people asked for their pay. Thus, when the rent came due or the marketing had to be done, it was my job to take care of that, because I was more concerned than the rest that the collective should function. I didn't realize until it was too late that this was impossible. *Beware* is about waking up and realizing you have dreamed of something that doesn't exist and that dreams can't always be made to come true. People were more concerned with their own security and having enough to eat than with the project that required their commitment. They worried more about the safety of their existence than about the project. For me it was the opposite.

Almost everything that is being discussed in the film comes out in simpleminded phrases. One character talks about integrating the crew into the film, making a political movie for the workers, but those are catchphrases that shouldn't be taken seriously. The character was modeled on one of my best friends. This guy had adopted certain leftist phrases in his vocabulary without taking them seriously. He avoided the dangerous consequences of his own words, but he used them to seduce people—like when he lured a Spanish worker into going to bed with him.

Your colleague Alexander Kluge has called Beware *a film about incest.*

Really? Does Dr. Kluge believe that? All my movies are about incest. My other films are just as much about myself and my life. *Gods of the Plague* is every bit as personal.

Work seems to be an important subject in most of your films. Many of your characters are troubled because they are out of work and thus cut off from reasonable contact with other people.

Work may be the only subject there is. What else? Most people work every day, and do it for fifty years, and they keep on working when they come home. Those people hardly have a private life to speak of. You might say work is their private life. The characters in my movies are broken people, for they have no work yet live in a world where they need to work. This destroys them. We live in a society where people must work to make a living, and many of my characters can't stand their work. As a result, they have nothing to sustain them and are doomed.

What would you do if you could not make movies?

No idea. When I finished school, I thought about that too, and I came to the conclusion that the way our society is structured, theater and film allow for the greatest measure of personal freedom. That is why I chose them. But today the most important question is: how to destroy that kind of society. If society is changed, people's consciousness will also change, but as long as everything is based on the principle that some must work so others can profit from that work, changing that situation is what it's all about.

Whity. 1970.
Günther Kaufmann,
Ulli Lommel

Whity

There is a black mother. Her son says, I don't want you to sing those songs. What songs? Black songs! The son is of mixed blood. Whity! An old man has remarried. His young wife is a hyena. People can be given injections that put them to sleep. Forever.

Two brothers, one is completely nuts, about the other you can't always tell. The old man is quick with the whip.

A girl sings in a Western saloon. The girl is beautiful. Whity loves the girl. What's the nigger doing here, someone says, and as he lies beaten up in the mud, he clutches the rose the girl has given him. He wears a light suit.

A woman cheats on her husband. Mexicans are stupid. "I love you," she says, and, "Hit me." Like most people around here, she has the capacity to enjoy pain.

Kill my father, a brother says. Whity nods. The blacks should be given more rights, makes them less inclined to get stupid ideas.

The other brother loves Whity. Whity beats him. Whity kisses him. There is a tenderness somewhere that doesn't exist in the heads of those people.

Davie must die.

The singer has a plan. Whity, go east! Whity says: Never. He loves his family.

They are right to beat you. Because you like it when they beat you.

A father whips his son. The son is a mute. His mouth is wide open, screaming. No sound. He lets himself be beaten for Davie. Madness!

One man shoots another man. A girl watches. It was an intrigue. This is not important, unless you need an intrigue.

And pain makes a woman say: Murderer. She says it in Spanish.

Ben is going to die. Kill Frank. Then the property will be ours. Property is always part of the reason.

I have a black son, maybe they know.

The strong torture the weak. Anyone need an intrigue, there are many. And flowers, and hatred. Why did you kill my father? Why didn't you kill Frank when I begged you?

I'm going to die soon. The will is signed: Ben Nathaniel Richard Nicholson.

You know why your father shot the Mexican? Booze and cards. And beautiful songs.

Whity kills four people. The father. The young woman. The two brothers. Where violence rules, only violence helps.

Whity and the girl will disappear.

RWF, 1971

Pioniere in Ingolstadt
(Recruits in Ingolstadt).
1970. Harry Baer

Backward into the Present
Harry Baer

Nothing is more important than to prepare settings for the next film. In the cutting room, Juliane sweats over the completion of *Querelle*, while I have the pleasant job of scouting locations for *I Am the Happiness of the Earth*.

For the "Discotheque" setting, I have already lined up the Song Parnass on Max-Weber-Platz in Munich, because the action can take place on two levels and several beautiful angles are available for the stationary cameras. The owner has no objections, and the price per shooting day is OK.

I Am the Happiness of the Earth will be about four people for whom life isn't going especially well. Yet they manage to come to terms with each other, make a life for themselves, and achieve happiness. And, for the first time in their lives, they are really in the money. The film's music is by Joachim Witt. We listen to it day in and day out.

The script is just an outline with some vague instructions, but for a seasoned team they make things pretty clear and explain what happens in this or that scene. The dialogue is given out the morning of the shoot, at the latest.

I have greater difficulties with the script's tenth setting, "Body-Building Studio." First off, the place on Dachauer Strasse that the choreographer Gackstetter shows me is pretty crummy. Second, I am supposed to act again in this film, at last, but only if I promise to take off some weight so that my muscles show again.

The sequence in the script reads: "Günther, Hanno, and Harry do body building. They don't understand why, with their intelligence, they can't make it as detectives."

With this new film Rainer is trying to prove that studio films need not be costly. Who says Fassbinder can do only projects that cost millions? Ridiculous! I'll show them! *Happiness of the Earth* is to be a low-budget film. Everyone gets paid the same. No problem, since all four parts are fairly big. Dolly Dollar plays the female lead. The film should be feasible at DM 500,000.

The shooting proceeds in an atmosphere of such exuberance that we sometimes wonder if this can be work. One scene in particular sticks in my mind. In the fitness studio I am being tortured on one of those infernal machines. The juice literally pours off my face. The other two aren't doing much better. After the sweaty ordeal, we are invited out for dinner. Dinner is hardly the word, though—a food orgy where everybody forgets their diet. Only a few takes are tough going. Rainer spares no one, though each of the actors has a completely different concept of the scene.

This year the German national soccer team is competing in Spain. The shooting has been scheduled so all important world championship games can be watched. Of course, every single one is considered important!

Italy ends up world champion, the German Federal Republic as vice–world champion for the second time. Serves them right, too, having wangled themselves into the finals with all those ties.

But then vice–world champion isn't all bad. One of Rainer's favorite games is reciting the names of the various players in the 1954 World Soccer Championship at Bern. Naturally, he always wins. Everybody knows that Toni Turek was the goalie, but Rainer wants to know the whole roster. Some of us don't get much farther than Fritz Walter. Here they are: Toni Turek, Jupp Posipal, Werner Kohlmeyer, Horst Eckel, Werner Liebrich, Karl Mai, Helmut Rahn, Maxl Morlock, Ottmar Walter, Fritz Walter, and Hans Schäfer. Germany won 3 to 2 over heavily favored Hungary.

This recalls the key reference at the end of *The Marriage of Maria Braun*. While her house explodes, on the soundtrack of the film the voice of sportscaster Herbert Zimmermann is heard: "That's it! That's it! The game is over! Germany is world champion!"

In *Veronika Voss*, too, there is a dialogue between Cornelia Froboess and Hilmar Thate about the Walter brothers. In another scene, the soundtrack carries a section of a game between Sweden and Germany in which Juskowski is ordered off the field. Rainer is interested in German history, and in soccer, too.

At the request of our "chief music director" Rainer Werner Fassbinder, I have started collecting music tapes from the sixties. Those from the seventies and eighties are going to the archive. We shall need them for atmosphere in the films we make in the nineties.

Rainer is devastated when he learns that Simmel's story *Hurrah, We're Still Alive* has already been filmed by Peter Zadek. He had finished a script and was talking with Bavaria Atelier.

There is much debate as to who should play Mitch in *A Streetcar Named Desire*. Rainer is staging the Tennessee Williams play for the theater and plans to send it on tour. In Kazan's film, Marlon Brando plays Blanche's vicious brother-in-law; Gottfried John plays him in Rainer's stage version, a belated reward for his performance of Reinhold in *Berlin Alexanderplatz*. Blanche Dubois is played by Elisabeth Volkmann, who was first seen in *Lili Marleen*, doing a breathtaking dance number on the floor for German soldiers in a beer hall. Next, in *Veronika Voss*, she played a serious journalist opposite Hilmar Thate. Blanche, a capricious neurotic, is trying to drown her sleazy past in alcohol. How Volkmann pulls this off on stage night after night is nothing short of brilliant. For comfort she turns to her sister Stella (Barbara Valentin). The production's premiere in Munich is a huge success, especially for the three main actors.

I have been appointed stage manager for the tour, which means that I have to supervise every evening performance between Flensburg and Konstanz. Being on the road with the actors, I am somewhat removed from the action. Maybe my attitude regarding the mass killings in various scenes of the gigantic Rosa Luxemburg project has rubbed Rainer the wrong way. We travel by bus all over Germany. Unfortunately, not as economically as I recall we did on other road productions, but in a sort of zigzag, following the performing schedule the tour director has cooked up. Often we have barely time to change our underwear as we speed to an opening in northern Germany, having just performed in the south. The converted rows of seats become our favored beds on the bus.

In this production, Rainer has obviously "forgotten" the things that can happen on the road. The way the two female protagonists are going at each other is a movie in itself. Liesel and Bärbel, eminently proficient at verbal back-and-forth, are driving not only the bus driver out of his mind.

At this time Rainer is writing his script for the film *Rosa L.* The producer has promised him an American star, Jane Fonda, for the title role! With all the fuss about Fonda, however, the part eventually goes back to a German. Jane announced she would bring her family and that she wanted to exercise a lot. Rather than going into aerobics, let alone jogging, Rainer settles for Hanna.

The production is gigantic. The highly elaborate locations take us to Prague, where with little trouble entire streets can be converted into pre–World War I Berlin. Almost all the interiors are shot in Berlin at the CCC-Studios.

For a while there is a pause in the film work. Rainer returns to an old pet project, *La Traviata*. He stages the opera in Zurich, and it is beautiful. Lisgreth Schmidt, Ingrid Caven's sister, whom Rainer greatly admires, sings Traviata. He naturally didn't let on that he would have much preferred if the locals had produced his own opera. It is tentatively titled *Cancer*. Willi [Peer Raben] is supposed to write the music.

Perhaps the discrepancy between the big money sheltered in Switzerland and the futile utopia that haunts Rainer's mind inspires him to write a script about the sixties. Hence, in 1980, a movie about the sixties is made. Rainer knows better than anyone else that people cannot live without dreams. But many are offended when he comes out and says so. He lands between all the chairs.

Horst Wendlandt came up with the great idea to make a film of Pitrigrilli's novel *Cocaine*. It happened in a posh gourmet restaurant in Munich. Rainer was totally happy and wanted to cast Ornella Muti, Romy Schneider, and Brad Davis for the main parts. But first he produced a script, which Horst simply finds much too long.

They finally agree that we should again scout for locations. If need be, we can cut later. I don't really mind that Rainer is allowed to fly to Brazil to look for locations. But a chill goes down my spine when I hear that he is taking the Concorde again. This is too much. I am really pissed and for days refuse to speak to anyone.

In the end, I am compensated with a beautiful trip to Italy. The locations in the south are sensational and both Rainer and Rolf Zehetbauer are pleased. A trip to a penal island off Capri is depressing, though. We are not the only passengers on the chartered boat. With us on board are real-life carabinieri with a prisoner. For security reasons they have shackled the poor devil's feet with weights to make sure he really drowns should he insist on jumping overboard.

The cells of the dungeon—I can't think of a better word—have such low ceilings that the unfortunate prisoners are unable to stand. Imagine being incarcerated in this place for even a couple of hours! And they kept lifers here!

Rainer finally films a slightly shortened version of the novel, and even Horst is pleased with its length and, naturally, with its worldwide success.

After that another of Rainer's pet projects gets its turn. *Der Mann im Jasmin*, by Unica Zürn. This is again a project for television. Conditions during production are like the novel's subtitle: "Impressions of Mental Illness."

Meanwhile Rainer has somewhat calmed down and no longer feels the need to churn out two or three films a year. He has no doubt that Germany will again win the world soccer championship in 1990, but in the end, he finds it a bit much. For by now things are happening in Germany that force him into action. He decides to shoot a short, sleazy movie about black marketeers around Berlin's Bahnhof Zoo, crooked little money changers and profiteers, plus a woman who must choose between love and politics and is bound to lose. Despite the dramatic events that accompany Germany's reunification, a timeless documentary emerges which only Rainer could have made.

In the countryside around Berlin, Rainer finds locations that inspire endless new projects. During our scouting expeditions on weekdays (when else?) we come full circle around the city. They produce a great number of possibilities for locations, especially in Fontane's Mark Brandenburg.

Rainer is back at work on a series on German history. But with the European soccer championships starting in Sweden on June 10, 1982, Rainer takes a leave of absence.

Rainer Werner Fassbinder
Juliane Lorenz

It is not thinking but dreaming that broadens life.

—RWF

Someone who has love in his belly won't have an easy time in this life.

But when he decides not to let this love wither on the vine, something beautiful may grow from it. For instance: a life between 1945 and 1982, and its artistic expression in what was then the Federal Republic of Germany.

When I first met Rainer in 1976, in an editing room of Bavaria Studios in Munich, I was young, studying during the day and working at night, and not at all experienced in either life or the business of film. I didn't know at that time that he would be the one who would most significantly influence and nurture my personal and professional development. Although I became more experienced in both ways, to this day there is no one to whom I owe a greater debt. There is no one to whom I have felt as close, or whose absence from this planet still fills me with profound sadness.

Rainer Werner Fassbinder left behind not only memories but a whole oeuvre, one that will outlast political fluctuations and changes. It tells of human beings and their feelings, their relationships to others in a society we call democratic. It shows that there are always more dreams, ideas, and interests beyond what this supposedly reasonable society will accept. Some can cope with its demands and contradictions; others can't.

With the exception of Fassbinder, hardly anyone in Germany has successfully approached these issues in literary or cinematographic terms—not just described them but confronted them in real-life situations.

Each film I edited for Rainer was an important one, and a challenge. Each time I see a Fassbinder film projected, no matter which one, I again feel at home and close.

Rainer once advised me not to read too much about an author or artist, but to look instead at his or her body of work. I should like to pass on this advice, which I have always considered extremely useful. I hope the viewers of these films will experience the same joy I had in this pursuit, or even perhaps rage at the thought that not too long ago there lived a man who not only expressed a great deal but also made things move; a man who swam against the tide of what was generally accepted and who, in the end, learned to persevere; a man who died much too young.

Querelle. 1982.
Jeanne Moreau

My Encounter with the Unknown Dancer
Jeanne Moreau

In my cinematic imagination, Jeanne Moreau is the embodiment of woman. And in this story, Lysiane is woman.

—RWF

Strangely enough, I knew the German film years before it was being discussed in France or the U.S.A., and I had contacts with many German filmmakers: Werner Schroeter, Daniel Schmid, and Wim Wenders, who belongs in a different category altogether and is closely connected to Handke. They all told me about this "enfant terrible," this unique person Fassbinder. I heard favorable opinions as well as the opposite. Personally, I only knew him through his movies and by reputation.

I heard he was planning to cast me for a part in *Querelle*. I had read *Querelle de Brest*, but that was long ago. Without thinking, I accepted on the spur of the moment. I was eager to work with him, get to know him, and this encounter . . . this mixture, this connection, Fassbinder/Genet. . . . I then reread the book and asked myself where I fitted into that story. That is a very normal reaction: who am I, who is this Lysiane?

Of course, if one examines the story, the spell it casts or the protagonist Querelle de Brest, Lysiane is the epitome of conventionality: together with her husband she owns a bar. She is the mistress of Querelle's brother; her husband gambles and wins: Querelle becomes his lover. Lysiane is completely caught up in this relationship. For no matter what a woman may say, her first thought is always that she has no place in this homosexual world where her femininity no longer dominates. I am quite familiar with the phenomenon of a dual personality. I am conscious of my own masculine traits and I also recognize feminine traits in men.

I felt rejected, though I had not even entered this universe and had no idea what I would do in the part of Lysiane. When it comes to that, I normally stop asking myself further questions.

Since I had been a close friend of Genet's in the early days, I called Monique Lange, a mutual friend. I asked her, do you know who Lysiane is, how, what, why. . . . We read entire passages to each other over the phone . . . and I realized that it wasn't getting me anywhere.

All that counted at the moment was Fassbinder, his vision of the part. I needed to wait.

It started with the costumes. Whenever I was supposed to meet Rainer, he was unable to come. I knew his entire staff, yet I didn't know him. To me he remained the invisible man. Gradually this became somewhat intriguing.

During my first visit to Berlin, I meet Barbara Baum; I am shown designs and samples of costumes. Everything has a nostalgic trend, I am given a girdle, lingerie, straps, and I think: "They must be kidding, all this macho style. . . ." First fitting. . . . On this occasion I learn that I am also supposed to sing two songs, two poems by Oscar Wilde from "The Ballad of Reading Gaol," which he published after he was released from jail. They were beautiful.

Indirectly, through costumes and poems, I formed a relationship with this man I didn't know and with the universe of his *Querelle*. I also learned that there would be no filming on location, though originally there had been a plan to shoot part of the movie in Brest. All sets had been built in a Berlin studio.

Once again I was invited to come to Berlin, this time to the Film Festival, as Rainer's film *Veronika Voss* had been selected for the competition. I asked the producer whether Rainer would be there, but he wasn't sure. So I tried my costumes and that night I attended the performance. I ask for Rainer. "He is on his way, we expect him, but we don't know if he'll come. . . ." I enter the movie theater, still no Rainer. . . . After a while, the producer, who keeps leaving his box, tells me: "Rainer has arrived, but he is terribly scared. . . ." That was incredible, because I had gotten into a panic myself.

The film ends; Rainer, surrounded by his staff, appears on stage, getting a warm reception. . . . In the bright spotlight he looks very handsome, he is well dressed . . . I had been told that he never wears a suit, that he had bought one just for the occasion, with a very flashy watch chain. . . . At last my presence is announced.

As we leave the auditorium, we suddenly find each other face to face, and, of course, we are unable to exchange a single word. So Rainer sends me a message, asking if I would like to join him later at a restaurant. I accept . . . and then we lose touch again; I get into one car, Rainer into another. . . . In the midst of an unbelievable crowd, we eventually meet again; naturally the photographers are trying to push me in his direction. But whenever we have a chance to talk, others intervene, besides I don't speak German all that well. At one point, I leave, numbed by the noise and hoping to see him the following day. But by then he has left.

The shooting begins. . . . I have been put up in a Berlin hotel, I practice my songs and ask Peer Raben, if. . . . "No," he replies, "Rainer is busy filming, he is not coming." Then I understand. I understand that he delegates assignments as soon as he trusts a person, whether with costumes or songs. . . . He gave people complete freedom. You always dealt with Rainer's staff, who knew precisely what he wanted and what he liked.

His death was dreadful. An incredible number of people worked with him, existed through him. He had many exceptional people on his staff. Those were crazy days, fourteen, fifteen hours, and in the highly charged atmosphere it was his energy that carried us through. It was unbelievable how rushed he was.

When we rehearsed the songs in the sound studios, Peer asked me if I wanted to see the sets. That suddenly threw me into a panic. I decided I wanted to see neither Fassbinder nor the sets before we started filming.

I was called and canceled again at the last minute. I got up, I prepared myself. But I still did not know who I was going to be. At one call I was told I wouldn't be filming that day. So it went, for two, three, four, eight days. Then, one morning, we were on. I ask which setup it is going to be. "No, no," I am told, "this is not in the script. It is a scene Rainer just dreamt up. It is about a vision during the scuffle between Querelle and his brother." At the studio I am shown my changing room and a costume I have never seen before. Barbara tells me: "You are the Virgin Mary. You'll be made up like Lysiane, you wear Lysiane's jewels, but you are the Virgin." Well, so be it. Almost paralyzed with shyness, I step as Holy Mary onto the set which has a strange aura about it. During the past four days the others have been filming that magnificent scuffle.

Rainer is there, wearing a white shirt. I am told: "Please, stand there, move down this way." All of a sudden, Rainer comes up to me, kisses my hand, and right away the shooting begins. I was surrounded by movie characters. One was Pontius Pilate, the other Judas . . . still another, covered with cuts and blood, carrying a cross and wearing a crown of thorns, represented Christ. . . . I was totally baffled. The atmosphere was magic. I didn't understand a thing, but I had a clear idea who Lysiane was. And now the film is finished, I can put what she is into words: she is Woman, the Virgin, lover, mother, child.

Rainer was thoroughly familiar with the script and had that freedom that comes from intimate knowledge. It was magic to watch him place the cameras, set up the takes, frame the shots, and make the whole thing come alive, even though the script itself was full of life. It was so fascinating that I never moved from location. Things worked very fast. Normally it takes a while to change the axis, change the lens . . . and the element of surprise is lost. With him things happened like lightning, everything moved at an incredible pace. . . . I never met anyone who filmed the way he did, at such speed.

As shooting progressed, I got a clearer idea of how Rainer perceived femininity: as a multilayered thing, a kind of well from which one draws strength and which at the same time is a constant threat, a two-faced thing.

By the way, he never gave me the slightest instruction. We communicated entirely by osmosis. No instruction ever, not a single prescribed gesture. He spoke German. I understood what he said, I got it exactly right . . . and sometimes he laughed and said: "You see, she doesn't speak a word of German, yet she understands everything."

This kind of deep understanding is not easy to explain. Between us there were moments of great intimacy, though it wasn't until the last day of shooting that we touched and actually spoke to each other. I saw the child in him, I felt affection for him, I cannot explain it in any other way. And although he is dead, although one cannot call him or see him, for me he is present. . . .

Although I had only met him recently, it was an incredible shock when I was told, at seven o'clock in the morning, that he was dead. His instant closeness was very strange. It was a form of love. . . . I found a parallel for this phenomenon which I confided to him. I told him he was my unknown dance partner. For it does happen that you go someplace where you don't know anyone and suddenly a man asks you to dance. You don't say a word and you dance with him in complete physical harmony, which isn't just sensual but almost meta-physical. And when it ends, you never forget the moment of this extraordinary dance.

For me the filming of *Querelle* was something like that. He knew that I love white roses, and he gave me two hundred white roses as a farewell present. To this day, I have kept the little note that was stuck in the bouquet. He presented me with the flowers at the very end of the shoot. A strange story.

Interview conducted by Jean-Marie Combettes and Jean-Pierre Joecker.

Volker Schlöndorff. *Baal.*
1969. Carla Aulaula, RWF

It Doesn't Pay to Be Nice
Volker Schlöndorff

It isn't easy for me to write about RWF, because he always was a challenge to me. Even physically. I eat and drink in moderation, never took
drugs, and before writing this, I climbed over the fence of a sports field
to run my 4000 meters. We could not have been more different from
one another.

In June 1969, I went with RWF for a checkup with the insurance
doctor. He confirmed that I had an athlete's heart and told RWF he
should not go on living the way he did. And Rainer had just started. He
was twenty-four, solidly built, and he certainly had a greater tolerance
for beer than I did. With some exercise, he easily could have brought
his weak heart, the nicotine-stressed lungs, and his flabby muscles
under control. I cautiously advised RWF to try, but he took his physical
condition as proof that time was running out. He had great plans. Later,
perhaps, the destruction of the body became another goal. But in the
beginning he saw it as the tribute a genius must pay.

Though he did not express it that way, he was convinced even then
that he was one of the chosen. He did not brag about it; on the contrary,
he was modest, just sure of himself, not given to doubt. This is how I
first saw him in *Anarchy in Bavaria* at the Kammerspiele. I liked the whole
antiteater group. It was an ensemble that acted and spoke differently from
the usual theater. They were like film on stage. That night he took us to a
movie theater on Thierschsstrasse, where, after the last performance,
he showed his first movie, *Love Is Colder Than Death*. Again the entire
group was present, on screen and in the cinema. At first it was not his
filmmaking that impressed me. It was those people—how and what
they spoke. I had been in Munich for five years and I had been in other
places—but I had never met such people. Were they artist-bohemians,
petit bourgeois, criminals, working class? Where did they come from?
So many of them, and all so greedy? Had he invented them?

I watched him shoot a film on the fourth floor of an apartment building in Lehel. Irm Herrmann stood with her back to the camera. She was
supposed to take something from a drawer in front of her and then
slowly turn around. Again and again RWF made her rehearse the sim-
plest gestures: folding back the embroidery, pulling out the drawer
with both hands, taking out an object (was it a pistol?), letting her left
arm hang alongside her body, and then turning toward the camera.

She got mixed up in the sequence of the gestures, held back tears,
repeated until she moved like a mechanized doll, her face frozen in shock.
RWF made her suffer relentlessly until he had her where he wanted her
to be. He punished with contempt and rewarded by periodically easing
the punishment.

That summer we were together day after day for several weeks:
first, two weeks of rehearsals, then three or four weeks shooting by the

Isar, on the Autobahn, on garbage dumps and in bars. He played Baal. Almost all the supporting parts were played by people of his group. I took over his cameraman, Dietrich Lohmann, and even a few members of his crew. He wanted to turn them into professionals and asked me to hire them. As paid help, so to speak. Now I understood much better what he had in mind, for most of them didn't have a clue, not about acting or about filmmaking. They were secretaries, cab drivers, shopkeepers, craftsmen, or nobody at all. He gave them jobs, suddenly addressed them as production assistant, prop person, or camera assistant, and forced them to live up to their titles. In time, most of them did—or disappeared. Having spent ten years learning the trade from scratch, I was both flabbergasted and fascinated, for at that time I was ready to discard the professional's rules RWF wanted to learn from me.

As I said, this was 1969. I had just failed in *Michael Kohlhaas* with a large American production and wanted out of the structures of the movie industry. In protest, I filmed *Baal* with a 16mm handheld camera, almost entirely with nonprofessionals, without well-known actors —RWF was not famous yet. He was on the opposite track: his ambition was to find a prominent international distributor and to launch his next film in the Mathaser, Munich's largest cinema. He closely watched what I was doing and how I did it—from the camera to the lights, to the sound, from the shooting schedule to the daily "rushes." He came to see the rushes and made his entire group look at the different versions in the editing room. It was a paid workshop. He took what he could get. He also took over some of "my" actors: above all Günther Kaufmann, also Marian Seydowski and Margarethe von Trotta, whom he met during the filming of *Baal*.

The only one he wasn't happy with was poor Sigi Graue. He was supposed to be his Ekart, his lover. He looked sleazy, all right, but unfortunately he could not speak. He was so awkward that even coaching didn't help. Like Rimbaud and Verlaine, they were sup-posed to make love by the banks of the Isar. RWF had long lost patience with the hopeless klutz. Nothing was being accomplished. But I patiently held on to the casting error. It was weakness. As RWF later often said: It doesn't pay to be nice.

While we were filming, he wrote and rehearsed *Katzelmacher*. At night, he memorized the long Brecht texts—in the bathtub; early in the morning, often at sunrise, he was on location. It wasn't easy for him even then. He seemed in a trance, but he never forgot a line, never had a slip of the tongue. No way that he could fail in anything. And he never lingered; if he showed up for a meal, he was gone after the last mouthful. Not to lose time by any means. He not only had many stories to tell, he also had to outrun all the directors who had been there before him and to catch up with the entire history of film. This is why he never wanted to work on a project for any length of time, but rather left it at the first attempt. He corrected himself from one movie to the next; rather than iron out the weaknesses in one picture, he would start out on the following one.

This was necessary also for financial reasons, because those first productions worked like the snowball system: the movie in progress was paid for with the money for the next project. At the beginning there was no bookkeeping. RWF inspected our company's minimal effort of paying income tax, health insurance, keeping accounts, etc., and rejected it as too complicated. He could not achieve his goal by working within the system. From his revolutionary days he had retained the notion that as an exception he was entitled to stay above the rules. He also felt entitled to everything in dealing with people, since he had rescued them from the mediocrity of their humdrum lives. It may sound outrageous; but he was right on both counts, and the members of his group were rewarded with glory. The question remains: how does a man acquire such self-confidence, the will and the strength to prevail, the ambition to win recognition under any conditions and right then and there, if possible?

I tried to get into the spirit of it, to overcome my doubts. I had written a screenplay with Gunter Rupp, *Nagasaki Transaction*, a melodrama about secretaries who bring down their bosses, about meat testers in the freezers of a Frankfurt slaughterhouse, and about a homosexual child killer. A stark mixture, not really my taste, but I was looking for a change. I gave it to RWF to read, saying that it was a draft that still needed a lot of work. I hoped for his input. But he wanted to do it the way it was—as an actor. I didn't have enough confidence in my own script, though.

The Sudden Wealth of the Poor People of Kombach blew onto my desk. I felt more comfortable with that. RWF took a minor part. I felt justified in having given up the Frankfurt project. He told me I was in a bad phase. He, on the other hand, was being fêted as the man of the future, awarded all the prizes of the Federal Republic and even had his first public success. "Right now you are down and I am up. Don't worry. These things change," he comforted me.

Over the next few years we frequently experienced these ups and downs. We rarely met, except at award ceremonies. Ten years later, *Germany in Autumn* brought us together once again. Together with Margarethe, I had been the one who had visited prisons, joined Red Help and committees on solitary confinement, etc. But it was he who felt persecuted and acted it out in the movie. At the time, I found this rather unpolitical and egocentric. Later I understood that having spent ten years living on the edge of German law, he knew more about persecution and antisocial behavior in the sense of Genet than I did with my highly respectable protest attitude. Meanwhile each of us, following his own nature, had gone such opposite ways that we had little to say to each other. I visited him in the studio during *Lili Marleen* and *Alexanderplatz*. I noticed that he directed and resolved with the sureness of a sleepwalker, that he was totally professional, aware of all the rules, yet completely free of routine. I still had my doubts. At any rate, he now discussed things with Margarethe. He also consulted with Alexander Kluge, which was OK by me. In brotherly understanding we had a beer together. I ate something, he smoked. That was it.

Lili Marleen. 1980.
Hanna Schygulla

How It All Began
Hanna Schygulla

He is still quite young, no more than three or four years old and already he has climbed a place that is strictly forbidden: the altar of a church. And he absolutely refuses to be taken down. That is typical of Rainer Werner Fassbinder.

And this, too, is typical: when a few years later he gets up in class to announce: "I'm leaving now. I'm bored." And the little girl from his grade, who rings his mother's doorbell one day and, with a polite curtsy, informs her that "Rainer isn't really as bad as everyone says." Her name is Marion—like the heroine of *Eight Hours Don't Make a Day*, his first television series ten years later . . . and I am the one who plays Marion.

I first met him at drama school, the boy with the pimpled face, incredibly shy and cocky at the same time, the look in his eyes a mixture of panther and velvet. It was by accident that I got into the same school. I had become bored at the university and someone with shining eyes told me about acting classes. An actress? Well, why not?

He landed there because he had failed the entrance exams at the Film Academy, he, who had always known that one day he would make movies. So he needed to learn some other way, by going to the movies twice or three times a day, and by becoming an actor, to which he brought a hell of a lot of talent, as he did to everything else.

We acted well together, he as Meckie Messer and I as Polly in a Fassbinder version of *Threepenny Opera*, in Bavarian dialect.

Whenever we acted together it was very physical. He pulls me, I fly into his arms, he pushes me away, I bend over backwards—and then I go down on my knees, as if for all eternity—or the other way around: each looking in another direction, staring into the distance . . . a totally different alphabet of gestures, gestures of love and rejection in a roundabout way.

Ever since our first encounter, our relationship has been roundabout. As I remember, when I first saw him at drama school, I thought: "This one doesn't like me." I was surprised when he let me know—indirectly, of course, through another person—that he really liked the way I had "played" my first scene in acting class. It was a scene from Goethe's *Die Wahlverwandtschaften*, a play which in those days I considered terribly old-fashioned. I played the amorous sister who, bent over her embroidery, tries to hide her forbidden love for her brother. How could this have made an impression on Rainer, who quite obviously was a rebel and an enfant terrible? I was really surprised.

When I left drama school prematurely (a few months had been enough to make me realize that I didn't want anything more to do with acting), I had not the faintest idea what role RWF would play in my life one day. Besides, I had once heard him say that he didn't want anything to do with Capricorns because they were the worst, and I am a Capricorn.

So I was astonished when a year later he came looking for me and found me. He, too, had left drama school prematurely and, more appropriately, had landed in an underground theater group. When one of the female leads had an accident, he suddenly remembered me, though not all that suddenly, as I learned much later, not until the end of the thirteen years of our working together. For, as he said, from the moment of our first encounter at school he had had "a sudden insight" that the girl I was then would one day be the star of his movies. And that he did not tell me directly either, but in a roundabout way, through the printed word.

I, too, had felt from the start that he was "my" director. Not that we had all that much in common. We did not enjoy the same kinds of pleasure, nor did we share the same opinions, except perhaps a profound preference for the labyrinth of contradictions . . . but we never discussed what we had in common nor the things that divided us. I can't remember ever having asked RWF exactly why love is "colder than death." To me it is the opposite.

On the whole, his directing worked without discussions and explanations. He did it with his charisma. Wherever he showed up, he immediately changed the mood, for better or worse. Like putting a negative into the developer, he made things appear that hadn't been visible before. Things that looked poisonous in the harsh light or hidden tenderness. When he appears on location, people murmur: "Watch out, here comes the magician! Let's hope he's in a good mood and doesn't need adrenalin."

Since RWF is also an actor, it is fun on occasion to act out a part for him. Before every take, he puts himself into the position of the camera and of the actors. He needs that to produce the images he has in his head, or rather, as in most cases, in hastily sketched, small black-and-white drawings . . . and while he paces the actors' paths, he lightly outlines what he wants, sometimes as a caricature, adding: "Maybe like this, or maybe not." And we are his puppets whom he can motivate to certain individual actions, for within the fabric of his material there is space, a certain nonchalance, where with all his manipulation he simply allows things to happen. Sometimes he will say: "One more time, please. To me this is too contrived." Or he goes to the opposite: "I don't like this. It's too natural, too normal." To Jeanne Moreau he simply says: "Just be great."

In the beginning, RWF always jumped around like a happy child whenever he succeeded in something he was shooting. Later he acquired the impassive predatory look of an emperor who allows himself the luxury of having his fantasies danced out before his eyes, both autocrat and slave, obsessed with living his life vicariously through films (which he calls a form of insanity), making movie after movie, nonstop, without pause. Perhaps behind it there is the boredom of a man who knows too well how to manipulate, who increasingly misses the unexpected.

But who can really look into another person? Deep inside, everyone carries his own secret, most likely even his own death. His body was found at night before a flickering television screen, surrounded by the tools of his trade—sheets of paper, pencils, screenplays in progress. In the end he worked on several projects at a time. Did he die so young because he was in such a rush, or did he rush so because he was destined to die young? In his last interview, just a few hours before his death and completely exhausted, he said: "Maybe one must pass through hell to arrive in a better world. . . ."

LIFE—a light at the end of the tunnel?

RWF shooting the
documentary
Theater in Trance, 1981

Hey, Rainer . . .
Wim Wenders

. . . when did I first see you?

I believe it was at the Bungalow, a bar on Turkenstrasse in Schwabing. In the back, two guys were flipping at a pinball machine. The front room had a jukebox. A few movie posters were on the wall. Wooden benches, wooden chairs, wooden tables, carved with names. Bungalow was a minimalist place.

I remember a girl dancing by herself in front of the jukebox. Miniskirt, curly pinned-up hair. Her name was Hanna. And the guy with the beer in his hand who stood there for hours, watching her, that was you. You were with a gang, and all of you were in the theater. I was with the other gang, the Munich "Sensibilists," film school students, filmmakers like Klaus Lemke, Rudolf Thome, or Martin Muller, and a few people who wrote for a tiny magazine called *Filmkritik*.

One day we heard that Rainer had made a movie, starring Hanna, with very little money and in a very short time. *Katzelmacher*. From here on we looked at you with different eyes, though aesthetically you didn't have much in common with the Sensibilists. But we were impressed: you had made a feature film! That was something which, at the time, most of us only dreamed of. Not for long, though, at least in my case.

Then, I remember, there were years when we met mainly at the Filmverlag der Autoren, working hard and in solidarity with fifteen other filmmakers, trying to set up a production and distribution company. It was the core of the New German Cinema, a purely organizational and practical interest group. Contrary to the directors of, say, the French New Wave, we were not bound together by an aesthetic or cultural program. In all those years, when we met and talked, not a word was ever said about film contents or film language.

Once, much later, we met in Hollywood during an Oscar ceremony. I don't remember what the two of us were doing there. There we stood in our tuxedos, somewhat lost, in some lobby; and in that faraway place we actually asked each other for the first time about our respective work.

And I remember another encounter, late at night in Munich at the Arri Cinema. You were going to show a handful of friends and acquaintances a movie you had just finished and were very proud of. We saw the working copy of *The Marriage Of Maria Braun* with the mix you had just done. By your standards, the movie was made with unusual care. It was obvious that you had been totally involved right to the end. I am saying this because some of your movies show that you did not supervise them to the end, that during editing or post-production you had already started work on your next project. This one bore your handwriting down to the last detail. After the movie, out in the rain, a small group was gathered around you, congratulating you, showing concern and feelings that were new to us all: for a moment there suddenly was the New German Cinema, a confirmed unit, its solidarity not just for a purpose.

The last time we met was in May 1982 during the Cannes Film Festival. I had asked a number of directors to come to a hotel room, where we had set up a camera and a Nagra, so that, alone with the equipment, they could say something about the future of the cinema. Late that morning, you were sitting at the bar of the Hotel Martinez, pale and alarmingly exhausted. I outlined the project and the questions for you. Then you went to the room upstairs. I saw only a few days later what you said and did by yourself before the camera. By the time I got around to editing *Chambre 666*, you were dead.

I remember arriving in Munich on the night train. As I stepped out, blinking, into the sun-flooded area outside the railroad station, I spotted the headlines on the newsstands, all announcing the same thing: Rainer Werner Fassbinder is dead. Incomprehensible as it seemed, at that moment it hit me that all of us should have realized long ago that you had been moving towards that goal for quite a while.

You have been dead ten years and ever since we have lived with this loss that will not diminish, on the contrary. We also miss the movies you would have made during those years.

So long.

Berlin, 3/6/92

Photograph Credits